Searching the Internet Made Simple

P.K.McBride

MADE SIMPLE
BOOKS

Made Simple
An imprint of Butterworth-Heinemann
Linacre House, Jordan Hill, Oxford OX2 8DP
A division of Reed Educational and Professional Publishing Ltd

Ɽ   A member of the Reed Elsevier plc group

OXFORD   BOSTON   JOHANNESBURG
MELBOURNE   NEW DELHI   SINGAPORE

First published 1998
© P.K.McBride 1998

TRADEMARKS/REGISTERED TRADEMARKS
Computer hardware and software brand names mentioned in this book are protected
by their respective trademarks and are acknowledged.

British Library Cataloguing in Publication Data
A catalogue record for this book is available from the British Library

ISBN 0 7506 3794 3

Typeset by P.K.McBride, Southampton

Archtype, Bash Casual, Cotswold and Gravity fonts from Advanced Graphics Ltd
Icons designed by Sarah Ward © 1994
Printed and bound in Great Britain by Scotprint, Musselburgh, Scotland

Contents

Preface

The Internet is a treasury packed with information, pictures – still and moving – music, news, computer resources from shareware and commercial games and serious software through to Clip Art and fonts. Using the Internet you can contact:

- most of the world's universities, to track down information in their academic databases;

- thousands of firms, both large and small, to view, read about or buy their products and services;

- millions of computers to download gigabytes of files from their open-access storage;

- many millions of people – perhaps the greatest resource of all!

The problem is finding any specific items in such a mass of data. This book aims to make it simple for you to search the Internet to find the information and resources that you want.

Tip

If you are need to know more about getting on-line, setting up and using Internet software, see:

The Internet Made Simple Full Colour Edition, ISBN 0 7506 3944 X

or

The Internet for Windows 95 Made Simple (revised and expanded second edition), ISBN 0 7506 3846 X.

1 Before you start

The Web and the Net

The Internet is vast and growing ever-more rapidly. It now links computers and networks in almost all of the world's universities and research institutions, many of its libraries, almost all of the major businesses and many smaller ones. Millions of individuals are also linked through the Net. Most of those organisations and many of the individuals provide information or services over the Net, and much of it is available to anyone. There are some areas which are not open to everyone – you may have to be a member of the organisation or a subscriber to a service to get in – and not all of it is free, but restrictions and charges are still the exception rather than the rule.

The Internet has no central controlling body – which is both good and bad. It is good because there has been no bureaucracy to hamper growth and limit creativity; bad because the lack of organisation means that there is no simple way to find anything in it – or even to know whether something is available through the Net! Don't worry! If something is out there, you can generally find it – you just have to know where and how to search.

The World Wide Web

The Web is one of several ways of interacting with the Internet, but it is by far the simplest and the most effective. As a result, the Web is now the most important part of the Internet. It is made up of uncountable numbers of pages – over 100 million at the last estimate – on computers scattered throughout the world. The pages are written in HTML (HyperText Markup Language) and carry **hypertext links** which weave the separate pages into the Web. Each page has an address, identifying the computer, directory and file. These addresses can be attached to words or

Tip

There are directories, full of organised sets of links, to start you off on any search and once you get into the Web, you will find that pages usually contain links to related pages – sometimes on the same computer, but often on other machines far away.

pictures in other Web pages and clicking on such a link makes the Web browser download the addressed page. All browsers can display formatted text and still images. A good modern browser will also be able to handle sounds, video clips and embedded programs written in one or more of the current Web programming languages – Java, JavaScript and ActiveX.

The attractive, multimedia nature of Web pages, combined with the ease with which you can move from page to page have made the Web the most successful part of the Internet – but it is not the only part. Other methods of accessing the Internet's resources existed before the Web was developed, and most of these are still important.

FTP sites

FTP stands for File Transfer Protocol and is the Internet's standard method of copying files. An FTP site is one where the host computers hold databases of files for downloading. Some of these hosts are run by software firms, offering new software, upgrades, bug-fixes, add-ons and information files; some are run by universities or ISPs (Internet Service Providers) who hold stores of shareware and data files.

You can access all the FTP sites through a Web browser, but there is also dedicated FTP software which you can use instead (see page 104).

Newsgroups

Newsgroups are places where enthusiasts and specialists exchange ideas (and files) about particular topics. There are currently over 20,000 newsgroups, which between them cater for just about every interest under the sun. Their articles contain information, discussions, files and tips on where to find files. As each group has a distinct focus, the chance are that you can find useful stuff in it. There will also be experts among the groups' membership who can be good sources of help and advice.

You can get dedicated software for accessing the newsgroups and reading – and writing – articles, but any reasonably modern browser will have its own news facilities that will do the job perfectly well.

Gopherspace

Until the Web came along, 'gophering' was the simplest way to find facts and files on the Internet. Sites and files were organised into a menu system, and accessed by special Gopher software which could display pictures and sounds as well as text files. The basic concepts were similar to those behind the Web, but without the same flexibility. For a file to be (easily) accessible, someone, somewhere would have to write it into an existing menu – creating bottlenecks. And the gopher display did not offer the same potential for innovation and impact that you can get with Web pages.

'Gopherspace' – the files within the gopher system – is now fully linked into the Web. Little new has been added to it in the last few years, but it is still a good source, particularly for academic information.

Tip

Searching newsgroups is covered in Chapter 8, but if you want to know more about using newsgroups, see *The Internet Made Simple Full Colour Edition* **(ISBN 0 7506 3944 X) or** *The Internet for Windows 95 Made Simple* **(ISBN 0 7506 3846 X).**

Zone name examples

com	commercial (US and international)
co	commercial (elsewhere)
edu	educational (US only)
ac	academic (non-US)
net	network provider
org	non-commercial organisation
gov	government
uk	United Kingdom
aus	Australia
ca	Canada
fr	France
ger	Germany
jp	Japan
it	Italy
sp	Spain

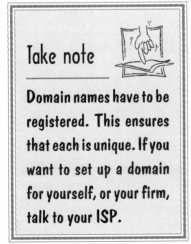

Take note

Domain names have to be registered. This ensures that each is unique. If you want to set up a domain for yourself, or your firm, talk to your ISP.

Every computer on the Internet has a site address, which consists of three or four parts, or **domains**, separated by dots. The last part identifies either the country (outside the US) or the type of organisation. The rest is usually derived from the name of the organisation. For example:

microsoft.com

Microsof, a *com*mercial organisation in the US.

bh.co.uk

*B*utterworth-*H*einemann, a *c*ompany in the *UK*.

gn.apc.org

*G*reen*N*et, a member of the *A*ssociation for *P*rogressive *C*ommunications *org*anisation.

ftp.sussex.ac.uk

The *ftp* server (file store) at *Sussex* University in the *UK*

URLs

Every site, file, page and person on the Internet has a URL – Uniform Resource Locator – which tells you what sort of thing it is, and where to find it. For example, the URL of the publisher's main page is:

http://www.bh.com/register/uk/index.htm

type of resource   site address   path to directory   filename

The first part of the URL tells you the type of the resource.

http: HyperText Transfer Protocol (Web page)

ftp: File Transfer Protocol (file or FTP site)

news: Newsgroup article

gopher: Gopher menu or document

mailto: E-mail address of a person

Web page and FTP URLs

These follow a similar pattern. The **site address** is always present – in fact, there may only be a site address:

http://www.yahoo.co.uk

It can also be written with a slash at the end – this simply marks it as the entry point to the site:

http://www.yahoo.co.uk/

Either of these will take you to the same place – the main page at Yahoo (see page 16).

A large site may divide its storage into **directories** – this is more common in FTP sites.

ftp://ftp.cica.indiana.edu/pub/pc/

This will take you into the *pc* sub-directory of *pub* at the FTP site at *Indiana* University in the US.

The URL of someone's home page will typically consist of the service provider's address followed by a tilde (~) and the person's username. This takes you to the top page of my set at TCP:

http://www.tcp.co.uk/~macbride

FTP files and Web pages – other than the top page – will have the filename at the end.

http://vlib.stanford.edu/Overview2.html

This is the URL of the contents page of the WWW Virtual Library (see page 34 for more on using this resource). Two important points arise from this example.

● **Case matters.** URLs generally only use lower-case letters, but if there are any capital letters in a URL, they must be typed as capitals.

● Web page names can end in either **.htm** or **.html**. If you are copying a URL, make sure you get it right!

Take note

Modern browsers can handle all types of **URL**.

news URLs

Newsgroups are organised into a hierarchy, and their URLs are derived directly from this. For example:

> **news://comp.graphics.apps.corel**

The **comp** section contains over 800 groups. One of its sub-divisions is **graphics**, which is again sub-divided. In its **apps** set, you will find this newsgroup, devoted to discussions about the **Corel** Draw graphics application.

A major problem about finding material in the newsgroups is that the organisation is not particularly thorough. For any given topic, there may be several groups in quite different parts of the system. There is another for Corel Draw users, for instance, at **alt.corel.graphics**. There is no guarantee of where a group will be located. You might have expected the Blackadder fans to have their group in **uk.media.tv**, but it is over in the massive alt section (nearly 3,000 groups) at **alt.comedy.british.blackadder**.

We'll look at how to find relevant groups in Chapter 8.

E-mail addresses

Almost all e-mail addresses follow the same format:

> **name@site.address**

But there is a lot of variation in the way that the name may be written. It is normally based on the person's real name, but may be their nickname, or include a number or code.

'Mary Jean Baker' might turn up on the Net as 'Mary.Baker', 'Mary_Baker', 'mjbaker', 'marylin', 'mjb123', or similar.

It is not always possible to find someone's e-mail address, but there are a number of avenues that are worth exploring. We'll turn to these in Chapter 7.

Tip

There are Made Simple books on Netscape and Internet Explorer, to help you to get the best from your browser.

What can you find?

Information

The Internet is a great source of information of all kinds. It is, not surprisingly, excellent for news, advice, technical reports and discussions about the Internet in particular and computing in general. It is very good for national and international news and weather forecasts, thanks to the many papers and broadcasters who also publish on-line. The quality and quantity of local news and information varies hugely – the coverage is far better in the US than elsewhere in the world – but is improving rapidly as local papers, libraries and councils realise the value of the Internet as a broadcasting medium.

As an academic resource, whether you are looking for homework answers or engaged in post-graduate research, it is something of a curate's egg. If you are lucky, you will find bucketsful of high-quality stuff; more likely you will find material at the same kind of level that would be in an encyclopedia; sometimes you will draw a blank.

Products and services

Again, the computing industry leads the field here. If you want technical specifications or reviews of any hardware or software, you can find it on-line. You can also buy it on-line, or track down your local suppliers. Financial services – banking, insurance, savings and mortgages – are also well-represented; you can research and deal on-line.

Internet shopping is growing rapidly, particularly in the areas of books, CDs, flowers and other gifts, but buy with care! There is no Mail Order Protection Scheme on the Internet, so deal only with established suppliers.

Take note

The Internet is a multi-media system. Much of its information is text, but there are also millions of pictures, photos, maps, video and sound clips.

People

Looking for long-lost friends or business contacts? If they have e-mail addresses you may be able to find them, though this is not always possible (see Chapter 7).

You can also find penfriends or other people who share your interests. Make new contacts through the newsgroups that cover your interests, through the people-finding sites or through one of the Internet's many penfriend organisations.

Companies

If a company has an Web site, you can find it easily through the Business section at Yahoo (see page 16) or most other Internet directories. UK business not yet on the Internet can be found through the Electronic Yellow Pages run by Yell (see page 68), while those in the US can be located through the Yellow Pages held at the people-finding sites.

Shareware and other software

There are gigabytes of files out there, just waiting for you to download! Much of it is free – and these are not just amateur offerings. Commercial software houses use the Internet to distribute updates and patches to their existing programs, plus demos and beta-tests of their new products.

The rest is mainly shareware (software which you can try for free, then pay a small fee if you want to continue to use it). Some of this is of very high quality – Netscape, the premier Web browser, is shareware.

Netscape

A good Web browser is the only tool that you really need for searching the Internet. With this you can find and download files, facts and other treasures, read news articles, and send e-mail.

Netscape Navigator is currently the most popular, and generally recognised as the best, of the browsers. At the time of writing, service providers were normally providing their users with version 2.0, but version 3.0 and 4.0 (Communicator) could be bought from Netscape. They all look and act much the same for most routine browsing operations, though the later versions do have additional facilities. All can handle Java applets and JavaScript code, though not ActiveX programs.

Up to version 3.0 Netscape is one program, but with three separate windows for the browser, mail and news. In Communicator, the software has been split into distinct programs – Navigator 4.0, the browser; Conference, for real-time audio conversations, with a shared screen; Collabra, for news groups; Messenger, for e-mail; and Netcaster, which lets you have financial, commercial and other news sent to you, rather than having to go for it yourself.

If you want to search the newsgroups, it is easier with Collabra than with the news window in earlier versions. If you are not that interested in the newsgroups, and don't want the extra facilities of Communicator, Netscape 3.0 takes less space on your hard disk and is faster to get running. Most of the research for this book was done using Netscape 3.0.

Programs in Web pages

❑ Some Web pages contain Java applets and other programmed elements. You can set your browser to ignore these, which saves download time and improves security, but you need to be able to run them to get the best out of some sites.

Java is a full programming language, and has become something of a standard for use on the Web. Java applets range from little flashy banners to full-scale site-navigation systems.

JavaScript is a Netscape development. Small chunks of JavaScript code are commonly used to make pages more active and interactive.

ActiveX is Microsoft's new programming language for the Web. It is not yet in widespread use.

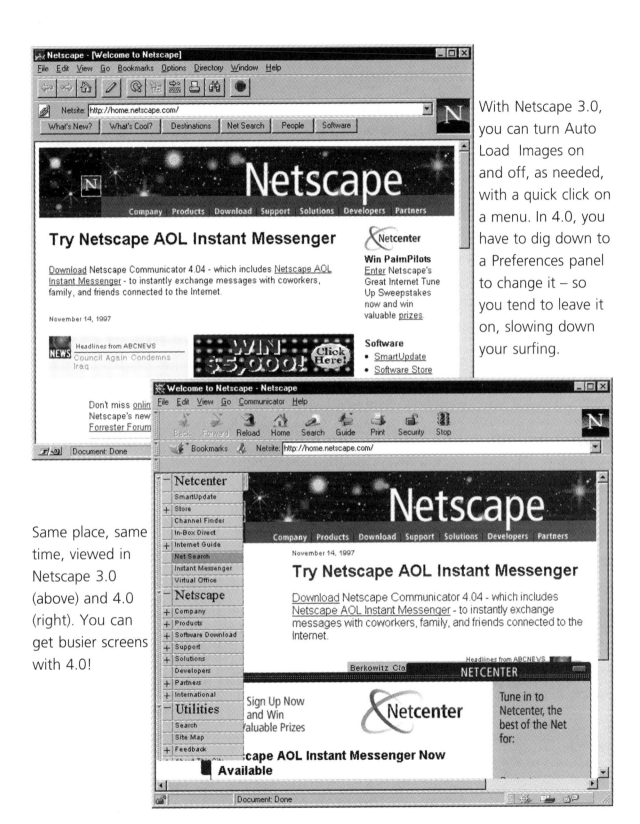

With Netscape 3.0, you can turn Auto Load Images on and off, as needed, with a quick click on a menu. In 4.0, you have to dig down to a Preferences panel to change it – so you tend to leave it on, slowing down your surfing.

Same place, same time, viewed in Netscape 3.0 (above) and 4.0 (right). You can get busier screens with 4.0!

Internet Explorer

Microsoft's Internet Explorer is currently the second most widely used browser. Its latest version, IE 4.0 (Windows 95 and NT only) is possibly easier to use than Netscape Navigator – especially for novices. It offers a very high level of integration with the rest of Windows 95 – you can literally reach the Internet from your desktop, and explore your own folders through IE 4.0. Its Wizards make it exceptionally easy to install and run, but it does rather take control of your system. For example, there is an automatic update feature which, unless you turn it off, will regularly check the Internet for updates to your software and download and install them for you.

The browser window has a feature which comes in very handy when you are searching. You can run the search and get the results in the left-hand panel. Click on a link there, and the page is displayed in the main area – leaving the results at hand on the left. This only works if you start from the Search button, and you have a limited choice of search engines and no access to their options – but that is often enough. We'll look more closely at this on page 86.

IE 4.0 can handle JavaScript code and ActiveX programs. It also runs Java applets – and significantly faster than Netscape Navigator can – but its Java system has been modified and is not standard, so not all applets will work. The other point to note about it before installing it on your system is that it is very large – anything up to 100Mb of space, depending upon which adds-on you select.

Take note

If you expect to spend a lot of time searching for and downloading files, there are special tools that will do these jobs better than a browser – see pages 104 and 108.

Tip

Internet Explorer is a good choice for family use as it has a Ratings facility. This allows you to filter out sites with an unacceptable level of sex and violence – you decide what is unacceptable.

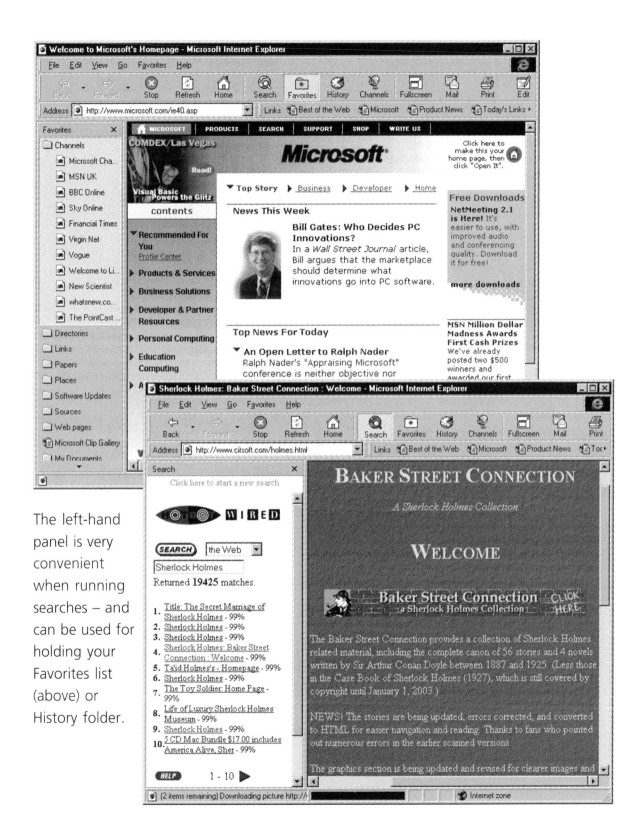

The left-hand panel is very convenient when running searches – and can be used for holding your Favorites list (above) or History folder.

Summary

- The **Internet** connects together millions of computers throughout the world. Once you are into the Net, you can reach any of the (public) files on these machines.

- The **World Wide Web** uses 'clickable' hypertext links to join together pages and files on Internet computers.

- Internet resources can also be accessed through **FTP**, **Newsgroups** and the **Gopher** system.

- Every site on the Internet has its own unique **address**. Every file has its own identifying **URL**. They must always be given exactly – there is no room for error.

- You can find information, products and services, people, companies, shareware and other software on the Internet.

- Netscape Navigator is the most popular **Web browser**, but Microsoft Internet Explorer is a good alternative.

2 Directories

Yahoo

Yahoo is one of the best places to start. It has more links than anywhere else, is well organised and cross-referenced. Start at:

http://www.yahoo.com   or   http://www.yahoo.co.uk

Expect to go through at least two, and probably four or more levels of menus to get to any real meat. The top level lists broad areas of interest with sub-categories. You can start from the main headings or go straight to the next level of menus.

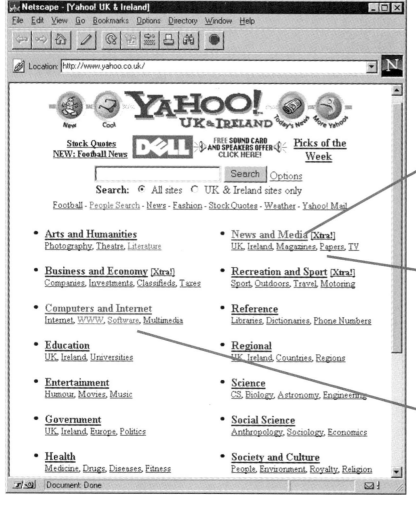

Yahoo categories

Arts and Humanities
Business and Economy
Computers and Internet
Education
Entertainment
Government
Health
News and Media
Recreation and Sport
Reference
Regional
Science
Social Science
Society and Culture

Click on a main heading to see the full list of categories in that area

An underline shows that text is a hypertext link – click on it to jump to the linked page

If the category you want is listed as a sub-heading, you can go straight to it

16

Menu pages

The contents of menu pages vary, but you will always find a Search box at the top (se the next page).

The central area lists related categories and those of the next level down. These may be followed by:

@ showing a cross-link to another menu structure.

A number showing how many links it has.

Beneath these are links to pages, with a brief description of each.

This is a fourth level menu – there are more cross-references than sub-categories at this level

If a page (outside Yahoo) consists purely of links to material relevant to the menu topic, rather than information, Yahoo stores it in Indices

Message Boards are areas where visitors can discuss topics – much the same as newsgroups, but inside Yahoo.

This menu page had over 100 links – many of them worth a visit.

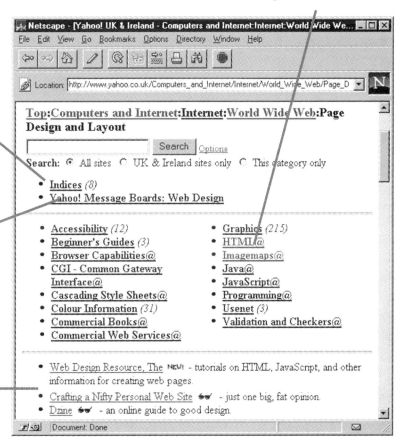

Searching Yahoo

If you are looking for information on a specific topic, organisation, artist, piece of software, or whatever, it is often quicker to search for it, than to work your way through menus or the descriptions of linked pages.

A successful search will give you a list of categories, if any, and a list of links that contain the given word(s).

Simple search

A simple search looks for pages that contain matches for all the words you enter(the *keys*), but treats the words as *substrings*. For instance, if you entered 'graphic software' it would look for pages with 'graphic', 'graphics' and 'graphical' and with 'software'.

- If you are in the UK, restrict the search to **UK & Ireland** only if you are looking for suppliers or societies, where being local is important.

- Restrict the search to **This category only** to reduce search times and cut out irrelevant material from other categories.

Basic steps

1 Enter one or more words to describe what you are looking for – try to be specific.

2 Restrict the search, if appropriate.

3 Click Search .

4 When the results appear, go to a Category to browse through a menu page of related links.

or

5 Work through the Sites and select from there.

6 If the search does not deliver the goods, click **Options** (see page 20).

Tip

The Yahoo menu structure is very good, but it isn't always obvious where you should start looking for a topic. Rather than hunt up and down the menus, run a search to find the category headings.

Tip

If you are looking for a company on the Web, start in the Business section and just type the main part of its name.

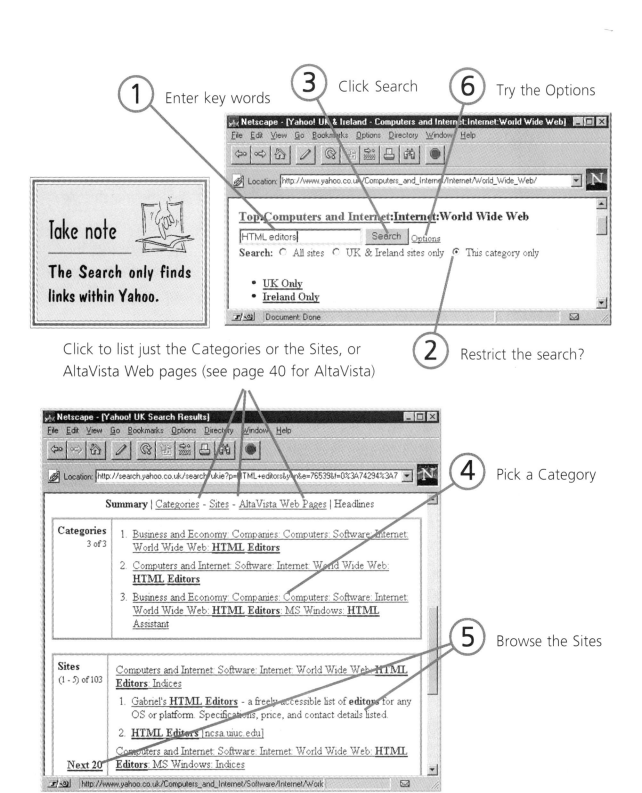

① Enter key words

③ Click Search

⑥ Try the Options

Take note

The Search only finds links within Yahoo.

Click to list just the Categories or the Sites, or AltaVista Web pages (see page 40 for AltaVista)

② Restrict the search?

④ Pick a Category

⑤ Browse the Sites

19

Search Options

With the Options, you can refine a search to focus on the most relevant material, or widen the search to bring more results into the net.

Match styles

- If your keywords are alternatives (e.g. Peking Beijing) then set it to **Matches on any word (OR)**.

- If you only want results that include all your key words, set it to **Matches on all words (AND)**.

- If the keyword could also be part of a larger, irrelevant word (e.g. 'lute' will also find 'flute', 'Klute', 'pollute') then set it to **An exact phrase match**.

Other options

You can search in **Yahoo**, in **Usenet** (for newsgroup articles) or for **e-mail addresses**. Within Yahoo, you can further restrict the search to **Categories**, **Sites** or **Today's News**.

If you are only interested in newer material, you can set a time limit, ranging from **1 day** to **6 months** – the default is during the past **3 years**.

The first page will always show a maximum of 5 results in each heading. You can specify the number to show on subsequent pages. Set this to 10 or less for a quicker response; or to a high number if you want to save the page as a file and examine the results at leisure, off-line.

Basic steps

1 Enter the key word(s).

2 Select the area to search – **Yahoo**, **Usenet** or **e-mail addresses**.

3 Set the **match style**.

4 If you are searching Yahoo, restrict the search if appropriate.

5 Set a **time limit**.

6 Set the number of **results per page**.

7 Click Search .

8 When the **Summary** results appear, switch to **Categories**, **Sites** or **AltaVista Web pages** if you want to focus on one of these.

Tip

Cut down your phone bills by saving long pages and reading them off-line.

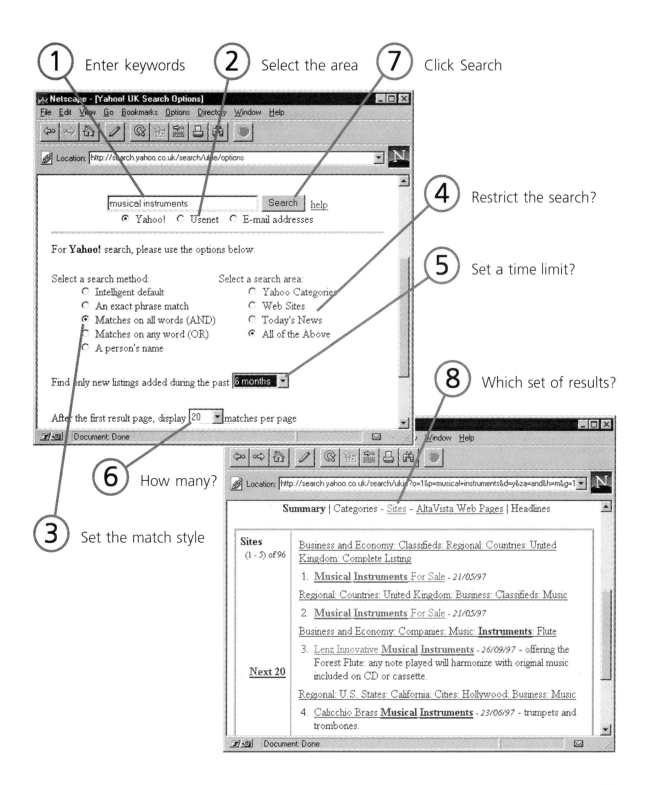

① Enter keywords

② Select the area

⑦ Click Search

④ Restrict the search?

⑤ Set a time limit?

⑧ Which set of results?

⑥ How many?

③ Set the match style

21

Excite

Excite is both a search engine (see page 57) and a directory. It lists 140,000 selected sites, of which 25,000 are reviewed – with the top 1% being checked and reviewed regularly. So, while you won't find as many links here as at Yahoo, they are likely to be more useful.

The content is geared to the home user, with good sources of information, but also plenty of links to commercial suppliers of goods and services. Layout is very clear, with an attractive magazine-style format on some pages.

Basic steps

1 Go to Excite at http://www.excite.com

2 Select a **Channel**.

3 Read the **News**.

Or

4 Go to the **Web sites**.

5 Go to a reviewed **Top Site** or pick a **Subtopic**.

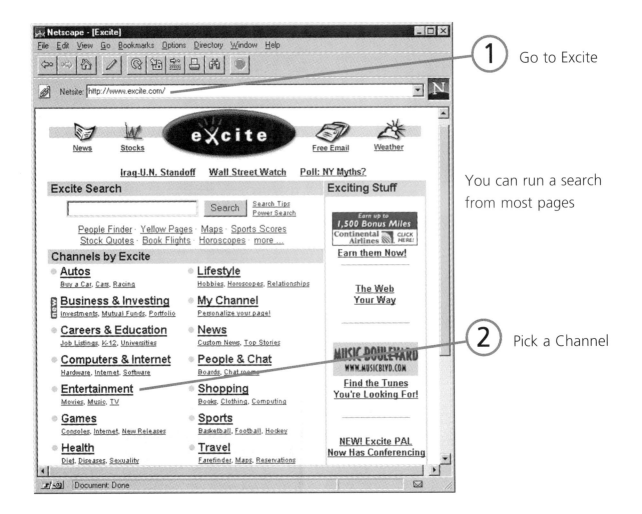

① Go to Excite

You can run a search from most pages

② Pick a Channel

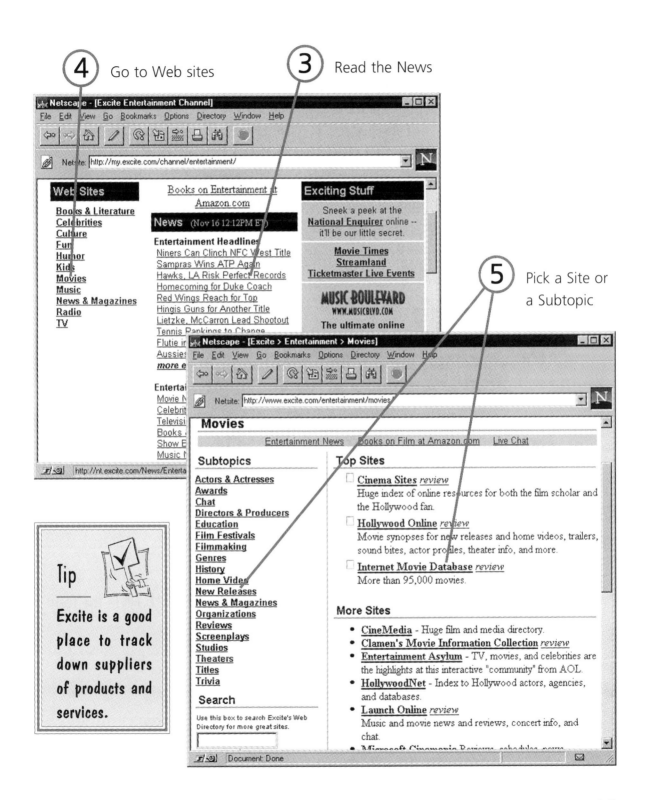

④ Go to Web sites

③ Read the News

⑤ Pick a Site or a Subtopic

Netscape - [Excite Entertainment Channel]

File Edit View Go Bookmarks Options Directory Window Help

Netsite: http://my.excite.com/channel/entertainment/

Web Sites

Books & Literature
Celebrities
Culture
Fun
Humor
Kids
Movies
Music
News & Magazines
Radio
TV

Books on Entertainment at Amazon.com

News (Nov 16 12:12PM ET)

Entertainment Headlines
Niners Can Clinch NFC West Title
Sampras Wins ATP Again
Hawks, LA Risk Perfect Records
Homecoming for Duke Coach
Red Wings Reach for Top
Hingis Guns for Another Title
Lietzke, McCarron Lead Shootout
Tennis Rankings to Change
Flutie in
Aussies
more e

Enterta
Movie N
Celebrit
Televisi
Books
Show E
Music N

Exciting Stuff

Sneek a peek at the **National Enquirer** online -- it'll be our little secret.

Movie Times
Streamland
Ticketmaster Live Events

MUSIC BOULEVARD
WWW.MUSICBLVD.COM
The ultimate online

http://nt.excite.com/News/Enterta

Netscape - [Excite > Entertainment > Movies]

File Edit View Go Bookmarks Options Directory Window Help

Netsite: http://www.excite.com/entertainment/movies

Movies

Entertainment News   Books on Film at Amazon.com   Live Chat

Subtopics

Actors & Actresses
Awards
Chat
Directors & Producers
Education
Film Festivals
Filmmaking
Genres
History
Home Video
New Releases
News & Magazines
Organizations
Reviews
Screenplays
Studios
Theaters
Titles
Trivia

Search

Use this box to search Excite's Web Directory for more great sites.

Top Sites

☐ **Cinema Sites** *review*
Huge index of online resources for both the film scholar and the Hollywood fan.

☐ **Hollywood Online** *review*
Movie synopses for new releases and home videos, trailers, sound bites, actor profiles, theater info, and more.

☐ **Internet Movie Database** *review*
More than 95,000 movies.

More Sites

- **CineMedia** - Huge film and media directory.
- **Clamen's Movie Information Collection** *review*
- **Entertainment Asylum** - TV, movies, and celebrities are the highlights at this interactive "community" from AOL.
- **HollywoodNet** - Index to Hollywood actors, agencies, and databases.
- **Launch Online** *review*
Music and movie news and reviews, concert info, and chat.
- **Microsoft Cinemania Reviews** - schedules, news.

Document: Done

Tip

Excite is a good place to track down suppliers of products and services.

My Channel

Excite, like most other directories and search sites, relies on advertising for its income – and rates depend upon readership. The personalised My Channel facility is one of the things that they hope will encourage you to keep coming back, and to spend more time there.

You can choose what topics to include on these pages, and set up your own selections of favourite links. The choices are stored on your computer, as a 'cookie' – coded data in Netscape's *cookie.txt* file, or Internet Explorer's *cookie* folder – so that they are in place when you revisit.

Basic steps

1 Go to Excite at
http://www.excite.com

2 Select **My Excite Channel**.

3 Fill in the form and click **Submit** to go to your personal Channel.

❏ **To edit your choices**

4 Click the section's **Change** button.

5 Edit your choices and links then click **Submit**.

Go to Excite

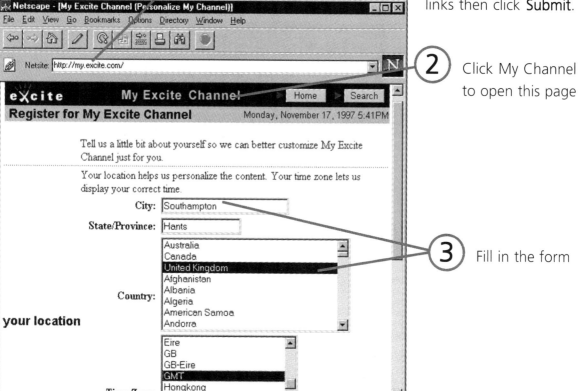

Click My Channel to open this page

Fill in the form

your location

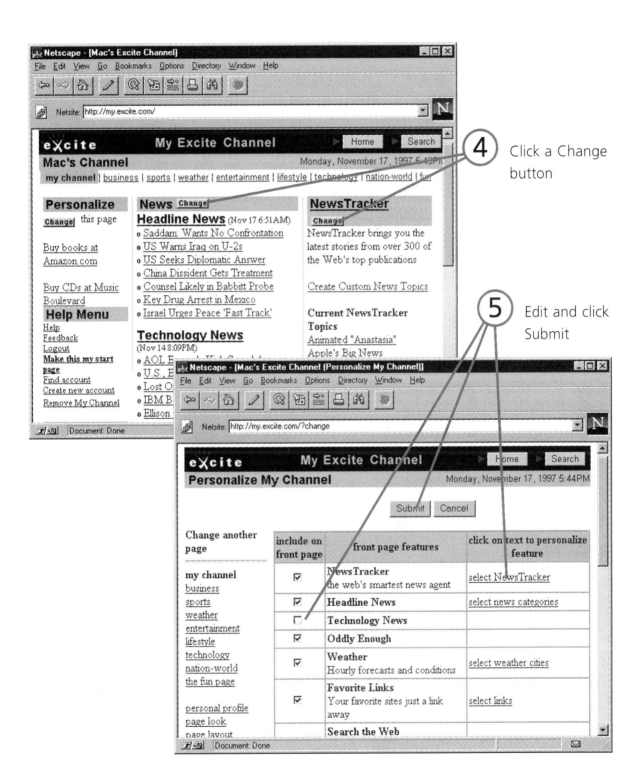

Click a Change button

Edit and click Submit

Lycos Top 5%

Lycos is one of the most popular sites on the Web, with a claimed 13+ million visitors a day! It is primarily a search engine – and we will return to this aspect on page 47 – but it also runs a directory of the Top 5% Sites, and offers a *Personal Guide* and other services.

Its Top 5% Sites are rated on content and/or design, and each link is accompanied by a brief review. So, although these cover only a small fraction of the Web, you can be reasonably sure that a site will be worth visiting and have what you want, before you link to it.

1 Go to Lycos Top 5% at
http://point.lycos.com

or

http://point-uk.lycos.com

2 Select a Topic.

3 Read through the list to find suitable sites

or

4 Click on a heading for a more specialised list.

or

5 Ask for a list sorted by Content, Design, Date or Alphabet.

① Go to Lycos Top 5% Sites

② Click on a Topic

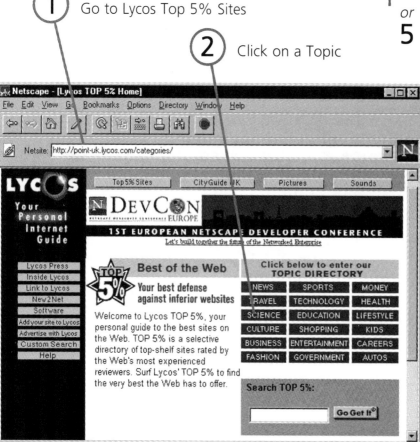

Tip

You can search the Top 5% from here – just type a key-word and click Go Get It!

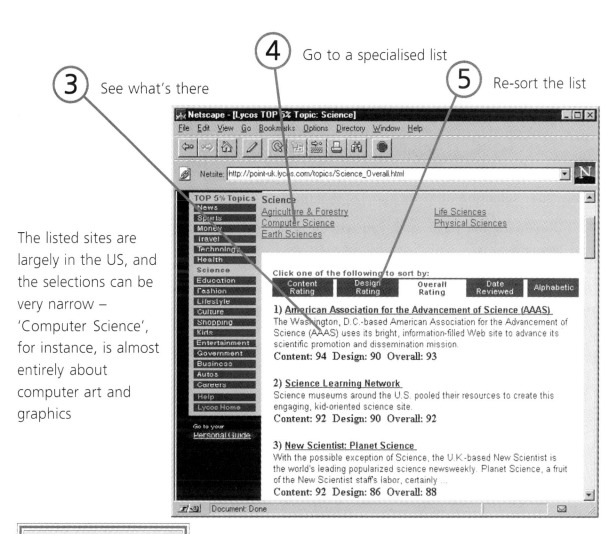

(4) Go to a specialised list

(3) See what's there

(5) Re-sort the list

The listed sites are largely in the US, and the selections can be very narrow – 'Computer Science', for instance, is almost entirely about computer art and graphics

Take note

If you live in the UK you get redirected to the UK version of the site.

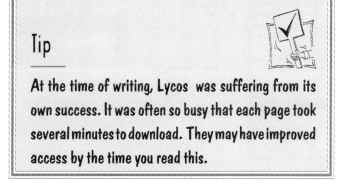

Tip

At the time of writing, Lycos was suffering from its own success. It was often so busy that each page took several minutes to download. They may have improved access by the time you read this.

Lycos Personal Guide

This is Lycos's equivalent to My Channel at Excite. There is more emphasis here on news than on links – though that does rather depend on how you set it up.

To start, click on a **Go to your Personal Guide** button – there's one on almost every Lycos page. On the first visit, you are asked for details about yourself and your interests. Next time that you visit, your Personal Guide page will havve your selection of News and Top 5% links.

● Bookmark the page, and you will be able to leap straight to it.

Take note

Lycos also offers other services, including Chat rooms, where you can meet and 'talk' (type) with other surfers, and databases of pictures and sounds.

You can edit the selections at any time

The **Stocks** display is almost impossible to remove!

Infoseek Channels

Infoseek, like Excite and Lycos, offers a search facility – and a very good one, as you will see on page 50. For the moment, let's have a look at its Channels.

The Channels form a hierarchical directory, like Yahoo, but with only two or three levels. Each Channel carries a set of 'Web sites' which hold sets of links and which are further sub-divided into Topics. The major Web sites are listed, along with the Channels, on the Infoseek home page. The rest are easily accessed at the next level.

Infoseek is at **http://www.infoseek.com**

as you will see on page 50

Tip

If you like using Infoseek, download its 'Desktop' software. This puts a slim Taskbar on your screen, giving you fast access to Infoseek's facilities.

You can also search through Companies here!

You can download Infoseek Desktop from the top page

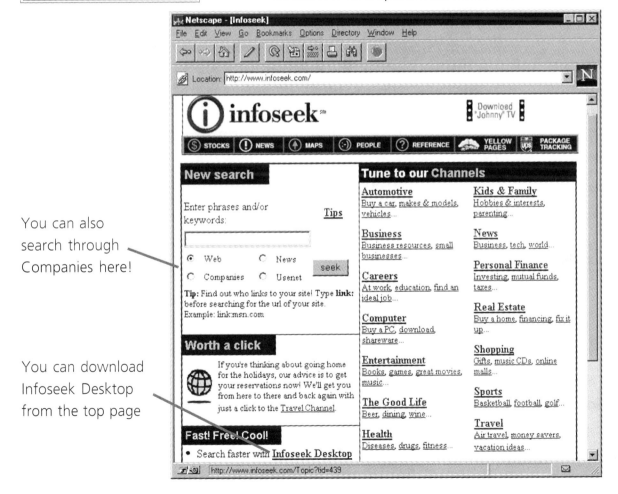

29

The contents of the Channels vary. There are normally some lead articles and News links, and there is always a set of links to their 'Web sites'. Some of those sites carry very many links – you will see a total of 383 in the screenshot of the Electronic Publishing topics below.

Tip

Infoseek is one of the more commercial sites. It's a great place to go shopping if you live in the US – and not too bad if you don't, as there are plenty of links to international and non-US companies.

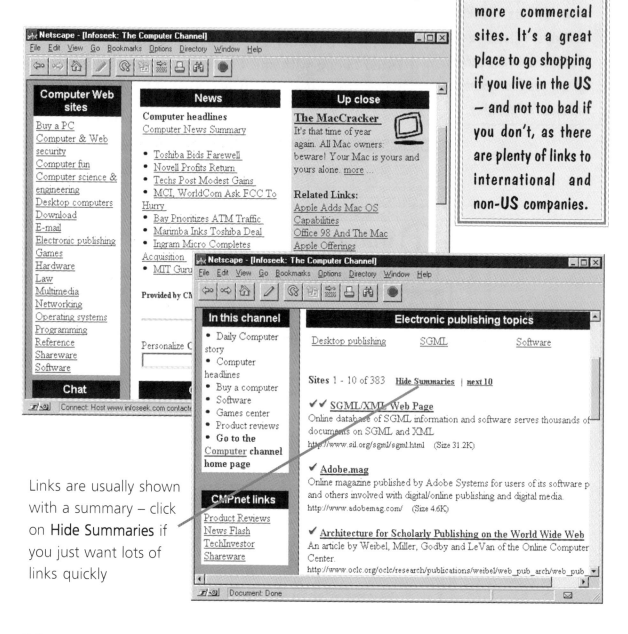

Links are usually shown with a summary – click on **Hide Summaries** if you just want lots of links quickly

Basic steps

1 Go to Starting Point at:
http://www.stpt.com

2 Select a **Category** from the sidebar or icons at the end of the page.

3 At the next level, pick a sub-category.

4 Browse through the links.

5 Click on a link.

Starting Point is a well-organised and easy-to-use directory. Particularly attractive features here are the brief but clear comments that accompany each link, and the presence of the main category list down the left of each page, so that you can switch to a new category without having to work your way back up the menu structure.

If you are looking for specific information, you can use Starting Point's Power Search. This links to major search engines to hunt down resources on the Web.

(1) Go to Starting Point

(2) Select a category

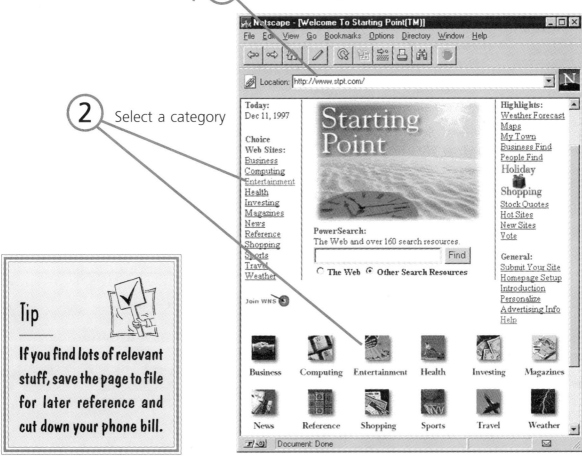

Tip

If you find lots of relevant stuff, save the page to file for later reference and cut down your phone bill.

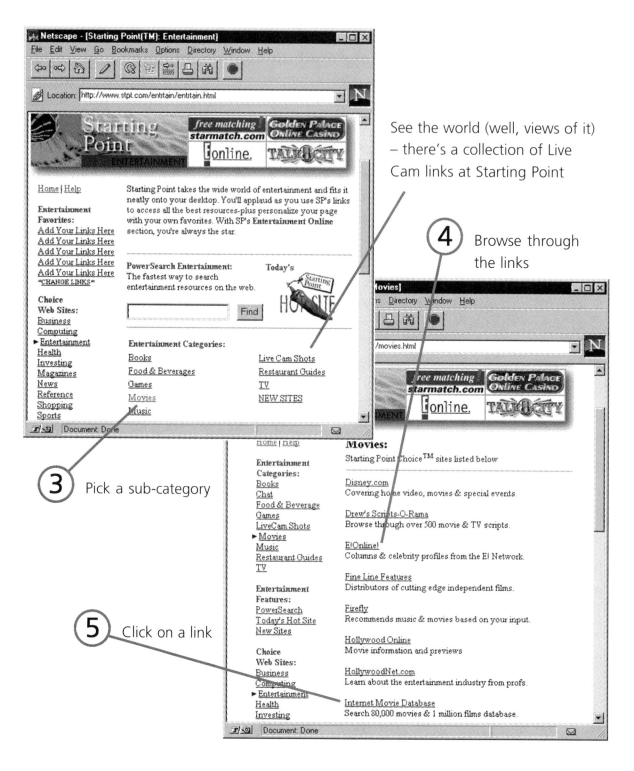

See the world (well, views of it) – there's a collection of Live Cam links at Starting Point

(4) Browse through the links

(3) Pick a sub-category

(5) Click on a link

The IMDb

Tip

If you want to go directly to the Internet Movie Database, it is at:

http://www.imdb.com

The Internet Movie Database (IMDb to its fans), is a great resource for movie buffs. It has the cast and credits of over 80,000 films – many with plot summaries, pictures and trivia. It's fully searchable and cross-referenced, so that you can find out who played a part in one film, then get a list of all the others they've been in – you can follow the careers of directors, cameramen, even make-up artists!

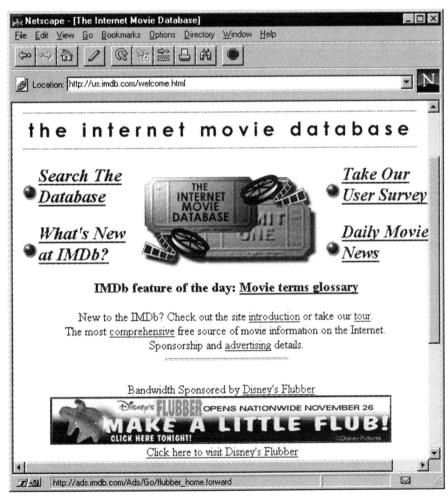

WWW Virtual Library

The World Wide Web Virtual Library is a unique resource. Its catalogue is organised by subject, much as any ordinary (book) library. The main structure is defined and the links in the Overview kept up to date by Stanford University, but its component parts are maintained by specialists scattered throughout the world. The result is an extremely useful resource, particularly for academic research – at any level.

1 Go to the Virtual Library start page at

http://vlib.stanford.edu/
Overview2.html

2 Scroll through the Overview and select a subject.

3 Read through the page to find the section on the topic you want.

4 Follow the links.

5 Use the Back button to return to the Library for more links.

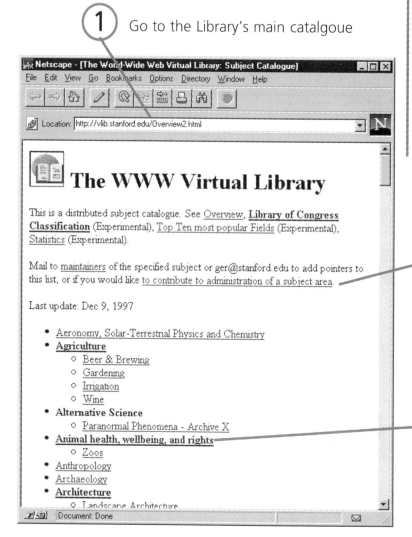

① Go to the Library's main catalgoue

If you are a specialist in a field that is not covered by the Library, why not volunteer to maintain a subject?

② Pick a subject

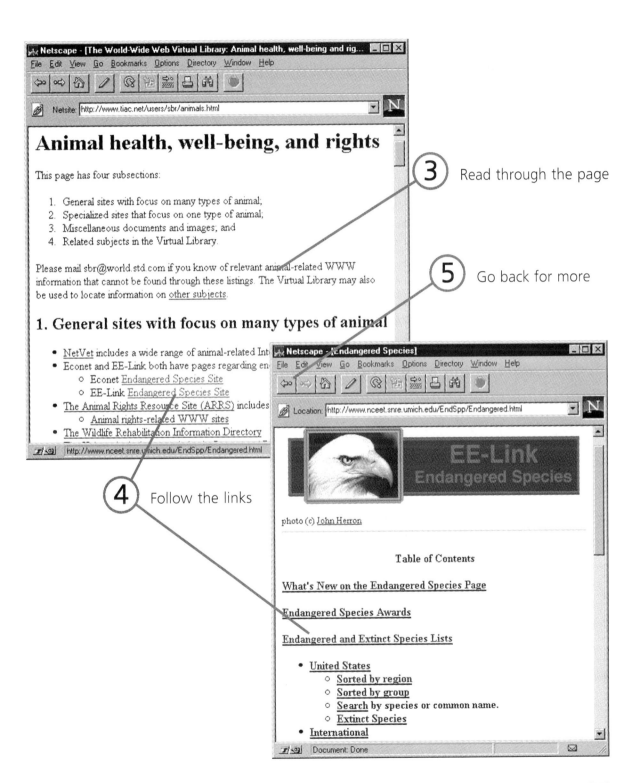

3 Read through the page

5 Go back for more

4 Follow the links

Summary

- **Yahoo** is probably the best directory on the Web, and is always a good place to start browsing.

- Searches at Yahoo will find any matching links within the site.

- **Excite** holds many links to reviewed sites, with the best being revisited and checked regularly.

- You can set up a **My Channel** page at Excite, to give simple access to your favourite links, selected news and other information.

- **Lycos** has selections of the **Top 5%** of sites, as well as a very large database. You can customise your own sets of links in the **Personal Guide** at Lycos.

- At **Infoseek**, links to sites and to related news stories are organised into topic-based **Channels**.

- The **Starting Point** directory is well organised and presented, making it simple to use – and it has some well-chosen sets of links.

- The **WWW Virtual Library** has its sets of links organised into subject areas, as in an ordinary library. It is a good place to start any academic research.

3 Search engines

Search techniques

Search engines vary, but the techniques that you must use to search their database are broadly similar.

Simple searches

If you enter a single word, then – as you would expect – the engines will search for that word. If you enter two or more words, there are several possible responses:

- Most engines will search for pages that contain any of the words, but display first those those contain all of the words. e.g. a search for 'Beijing Peking' would find pages with references to the capital of China, however it was spelt. A search for 'graphics conversion software' would find all those pages containing the word 'graphics', plus those containing 'conversion' and those containing 'software' – and the total could run to millions. However, pages containing all three words – though not necessarily in that order, or related to each other – would be among the first results displayed.

- Some engines will only return those pages that contain all of the given words.

- If the given words are enclosed in "double quotes", most engines will search only for that phrase. Look for "greenhouse effect" and you should find stuff on global warming, and not get pages on gardening!

Plurals and other endings

Some engines automatically truncate and extend words to cater for different possible endings. With these, a search for '**musi**cals' would also find 'music' and 'musicians'.

Advanced searches

These are much more varied than simple searches. Most support the use of logical operators.

Logical operators

Also known as Boolean operators, these can be used to link keywords. They are normally written in capitals.

> AND every word must match to produce a hit
>
> OR any matching word will produce a hit.
>
> NOT ignore pages containing this word

If you use a mixture of operators, they will normally be evaluated in the order NOT, AND then OR, e.g.

> boat AND sail OR yacht

will find pages with references to boats where sails are also mentioned, or to yachts.

> boat AND sail OR paddle

will again find references to sailing boats, but will also pick up all 'paddle' pages – whether they relate to boats or not. This can be changed by putting round brackets () around the part you want to evaluate first. So, to find paddle boats or sail boats, you would need:

> boat AND (sail OR paddle)

Include/exclude

Some engines will allow the use of the modifiers + (include) and –(exclude). Keywords marked + must be present for a page to match; pages containing keywords marked with – are to be ignored. e.g.

> +"Tom Jones" Fielding –song

Should find pages about the book by Henry Fielding, but ignore the singer's fan clubs.

Tip

If you enter words only in lower case, most engines will ignore case when matching – so 'windows' also finds 'Windows'.

If you use capital initials, most engines will return only those pages with matching capitals, so that 'Gates' will find the boss of Microsoft, but ignore garden portals.

Words written entirely in capitals will rarely find anything!

AltaVista

AltaVista is regarded by many people as the king of the search engines. It's certainly very fast and has a huge database! Unless you are looking for something rare, a simple search can produce thousands of hits. There are three ways to focus a search – use the Advanced Search, the *Way-cool topics map*, or Refine the results. We'll try refining first.

In this example, the search is sites that bring together potential pen friends – and we're looking for contacts for the kids! We'll start with 'pen friends' as the keywords.

1 Go to AltaVista at: http://altavista.digital.com

2 Set the **Search** area – the Web or Usenet newsgroups

3 Select the **language**.

4 Enter the keywords.

5 Click **Search**.

6 If you get a reasonable number of hits, follow the most likely links.

Otherwise...

1 Got to AltaVista

2 Set the Search area

3 Select the language

4 Type keyword(s)

5 Click Search

7 Click **Refine**.

8 Go through the list of topics, setting each one to **Require** or **Exclude** or ... if it doesn't matter.

9 Click **Search** again.

❑ You can Refine the search again to trim the list further.

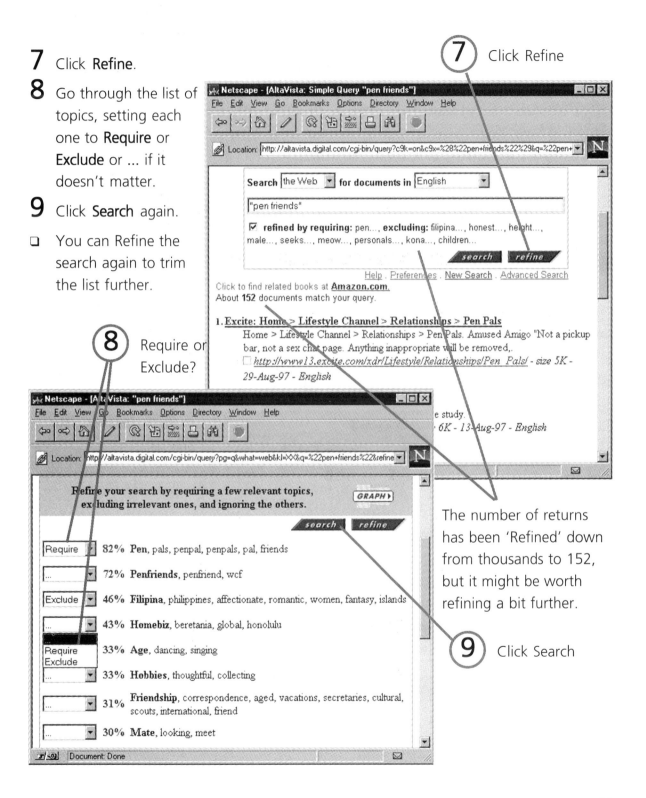

⑦ Click Refine

⑧ Require or Exclude?

The number of returns has been 'Refined' down from thousands to 152, but it might be worth refining a bit further.

⑨ Click Search

AltaVista's Way-cool topics map

Now here's a different approach. This can be great if you are not entirely sure how to describe what you want to find. It displays a set of (not always!) related topics, with options in each. You can select words from the topic lists to add to your keywords, then rerun the search.

Basic steps

❑ **Way-cool topics map**

1 Point to each heading.

2 If you find a useful word in the list, click on it to add it to your keywords.

3 Click **Submit**.

③ Click Submit

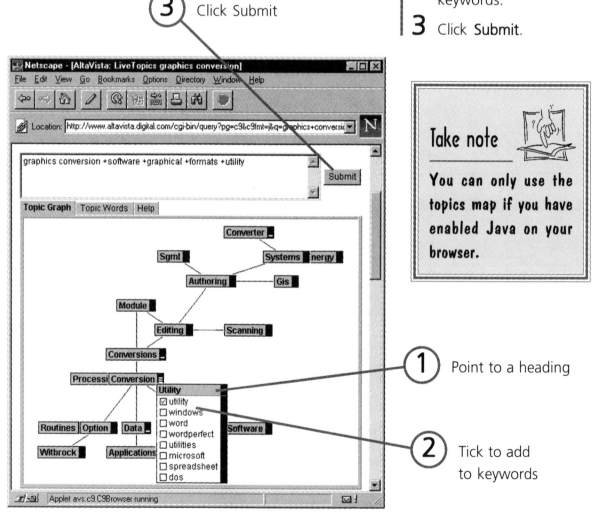

① Point to a heading

② Tick to add to keywords

Take note

You can only use the topics map if you have enabled Java on your browser.

Basic steps

Advanced Search

❑ **Advanced Search**

1 Type your keywords using AND, OR, NOT and NEAR to link them, as appropriate.

2 Enter the most crucial keywords in the **Ranking** textbox.

3 Set the dates if you want to restrict the search to certain limits.

4 Click **Search**.

AltaVista supports the usual logical operators **AND**, **OR**, and **NOT**, and the +/– modifiers.Note these special points about AltaVista advanced searches:

● You can link two words with **NEAR** to insists that they should be within the same block of text.

● If you want to accept plurals or other endings to words, add an asterisk (*) after the core word.

● You can set date limits so that only it only returns pages created between certain dates, or from a set date until now.

● If you enter words in the **Ranking** textbox, pages containing them will be listed first. This is of limited value, as it tends to override the main search expression.

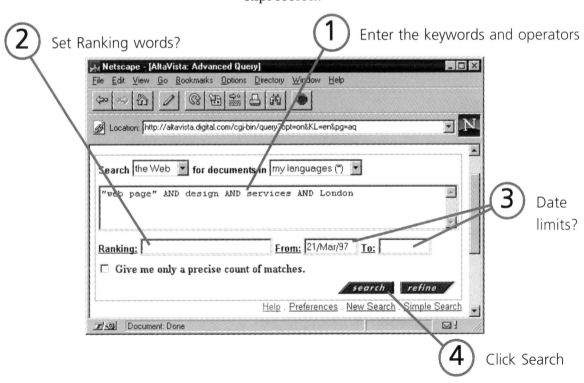

② Set Ranking words?

① Enter the keywords and operators

③ Date limits?

④ Click Search

HotBot

By the end of 1997, HotBot had indexed nearly 60 million sites. Searching this vast database can produce enormous sets of hits, but the drop-down menus on the interface page make it easy to set up a clearly focused search.

Type of search

all the words – the same as linking with AND.

any of the words – use when you are giving alternative spellings.

exact phrase – quotes are not needed.

Boolean phrase – select this if you want to write a complex search, using the AND, OR and NOT operators.

The search can also be for a person or page title.

Date

For newer pages only, turn this on and set the limit – from one week to two years.

Where to search

This is another optional setting. Use it if you only want pages from a certain country or type of organisation in the US; e.g. if you are hunting for US government information, you would restrict the search to **North America (.gov)**.

Results display

How much detail do you want? When in doubt, select **brief descriptions** – URLs only is rarely much use.

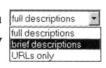

Basic steps

1 Go to HotBot at:
  http://www.hotbot.com

2 Set the **look for** type.

3 Enter the keywords.

4 If you want only newer pages, tick the **Date** checkbox and set the limit.

5 If you want to restrict the search to a Continent (or to types of organisations in the US), tick the checkbox and select the area.

6 Set the number of results per page, and the amount of information to be displayed.

7 Click **Search**.

Take note

You can also search for images, sounds and video clips – just set the Media options.

44

① Go to HotBot

② Select the type

③ Enter the keywords

⑦ Click Search

④ Recent only?

⑤ Restrict area?

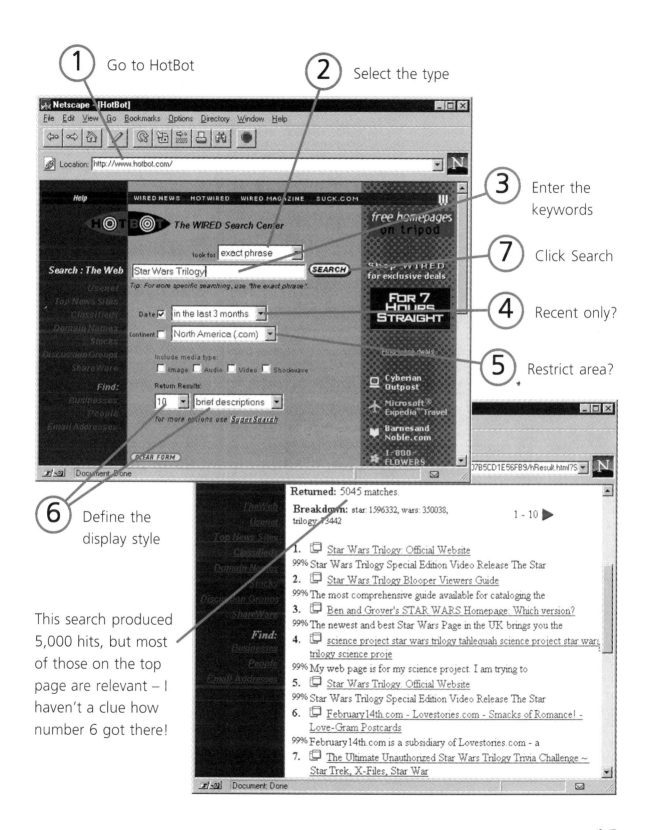

⑥ Define the display style

This search produced 5,000 hits, but most of those on the top page are relevant – I haven't a clue how number 6 got there!

45

The HotBot Super Search

If you want to, you can set up a more complex search at HotBot on their Super Search page. This allows you to:

- specify words that a page **must** or **must not contain**

- set a **Before** or **After** date limit

- define a **domain** or **Web site** to search

- include a wider range of **media type**.

1 Click **Super Search** at HotBot.

2 Set up the basic search as normal.

3 Enter the words that pages must and/or must not contain.

4 Set an **in the last ...** or **Before/After** date limit.

5 Enter a **domain/Web site** name or select from the **Continent** list.

6 Tick the media types to include.

7 Click **Search**.

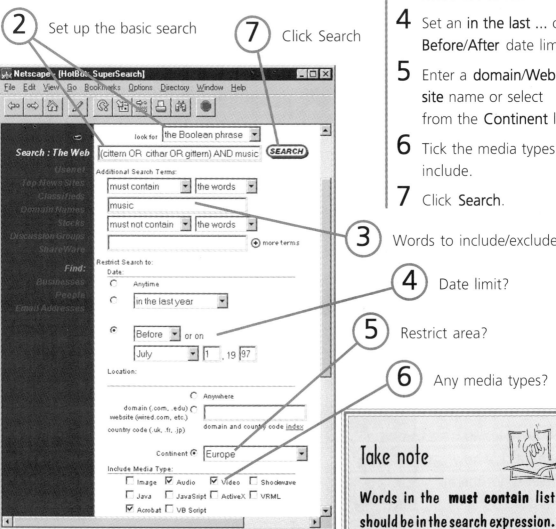

② Set up the basic search

⑦ Click Search

③ Words to include/exclude?

④ Date limit?

⑤ Restrict area?

⑥ Any media types?

Take note

Words in the **must contain** list should be in the search expression.

Basic steps

1 Go to Lycos at:
http://www-uk.lycos.com

2 Select the **Search** area.

3 Enter the word(s) in the **for** slot.

4 Set the **Find** option – all, any or the exact phrase.

5 Click `Go Get It`.

The Lycos catalog holds the URLs of over 55 million pages – more than 90% of the Web. Around 20 million pages have been indexed on their headings, key words and first twenty lines of text. Over 5 million graphics, sounds and programs files are also indexed.

Lycos normally truncates search words, so that alternative endings are matched, e.g. 'graphics' will also find 'graphic' and 'graphical'. You can prevent this by putting a dot after the word. Thus, 'graphics.' will only match 'graphics'.

The simple search has two main options. You can select:

● where to search – including **The Web** (the main index), the **UK and Ireland only**, **Pictures** and **Sounds**.

● how your search text should be treated – matching **all words** (AND), **any words** (OR) or **the exact phrase**.

1 Go to Lycos

2 Search where?

3 Enter the keywords

5 Go get it!

4 Set the match style

47

Lycos Pro Search

If a simple search returns too many hits – or not enough – try the Lycos Pro Search page. You can define your search either by using the options, or by writing more complex expressions – or by a combination of the two. The options are simplest to use, and will generally do the job.

Options

● There are five variations to 'All the words'. As you go from the basic match, through 'Good' to 'Strong', the match style tightens up, allowing less variation to the words.

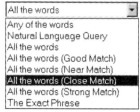

● In the lower panel, you can set the relative importance of where and how words appear in the pages.

Search expressions

The search expression can include the +/– symbols to insist that a word is present or not present on a page. You can also use Boolean (logical) operators to link the words. As well as the usual AND, OR, NOT, Lycos Pro supports:

● **BEFORE** – the first word must appear somewhere before the second;

● **ADJ** – the words must be ADJacent to each other;

● **NEAR** – the words must be within 25 words of each other;

● **FAR** – they must be at least 25 words apart.

Basic steps

1 Select **Advanced Search** from the top page or go direct to Lycos Pro at:
http://lycospro.lycos.com

2 Select the **Search** area.

3 Select the type of match from the **for** list.

4 Enter the search words or expression.

5 Set the number of hits and level of detail.

6 Set the importance level for where words apear on pages and in relation to each other.

7 Click `Go Get It`.

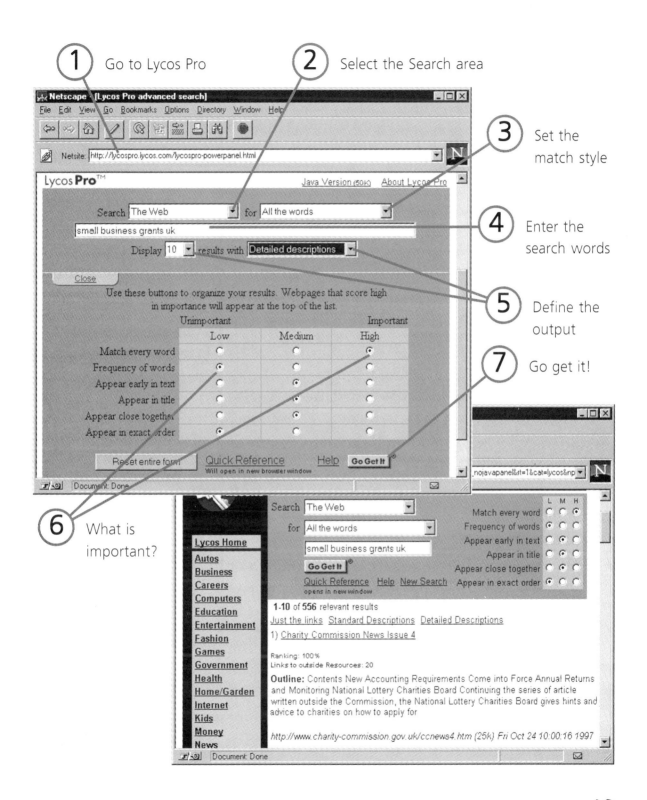

① Go to Lycos Pro

② Select the Search area

③ Set the match style

④ Enter the search words

⑤ Define the output

⑥ What is important?

⑦ Go get it!

Infoseek

Infoseek does full-text searching on over 30 million sites, and it offers an unusual, but brilliantly simple, way to search the Internet. When you get a set of results, you can search through those results – and do so to as many levels you like – so that you focus in on what you want. Instead of struggling to write one complex search expression, you simply give another defining word or set of words at each stage.

In the example, I'm looking for photographs of volcanoes in Hawaii, using the search words 'volcano', then 'Hawaii' and finally 'photo'.

● If you give several words, Infoseek will try to match any of them – e.g. 'mule donkey ass' will find any long-eared beast of burden.

● If you are searching for people, capitalise the names – e.g. 'Bill Gates' will find references to the man; 'bill gates' will find pages on birds, invoicing systems, logic chips and garden entrances.

● For phrase searching, enclose the words in "quotes" or link-them-with-hypens. "Quoted phrases" also match any capitals.

● You can also search through the latest News stories, or through the Usenet newsgroups, or for company information on nearly 50,000 firms in the US.

Basic steps

1 Go to Infoseek at:

http://www.infoseek.com

2 Enter the search word(s).

3 Select the **Web**, **News**, **Companies** or **Usenet**.

4 Click [seek].

5 If there are too many results, enter the word(s) to narrow the search.

6 Click [Search These Results].

or

7 If you are not finding what you want, go back and try another search word.

8 Repeat steps 5 to 7 until you have a small, but relevant, set of results.

Take note

If you really want to, you can write search expressions containing logical operators – read the **Tips** at Infoseek to find out how.

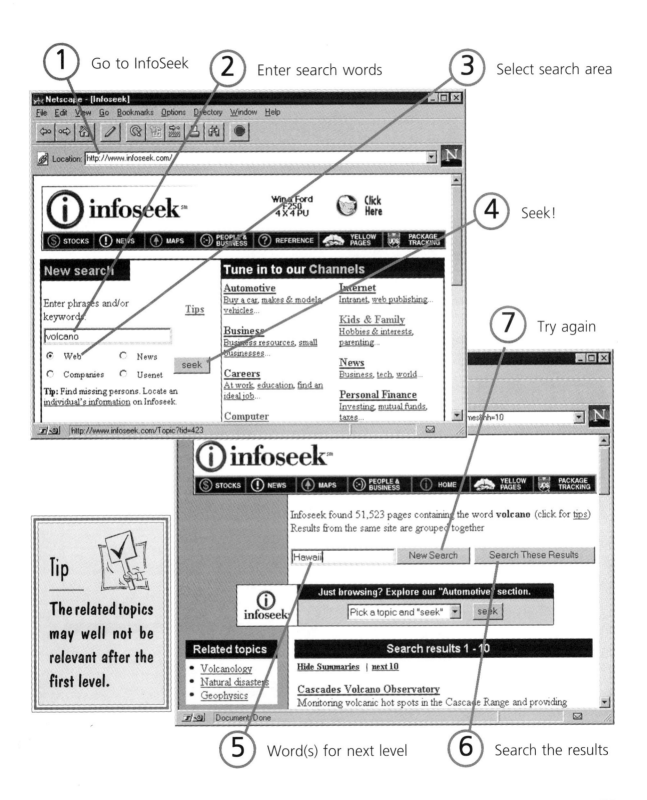

① Go to InfoSeek
② Enter search words
③ Select search area
④ Seek!
⑦ Try again
⑤ Word(s) for next level
⑥ Search the results

Tip

The related topics may well not be relevant after the first level.

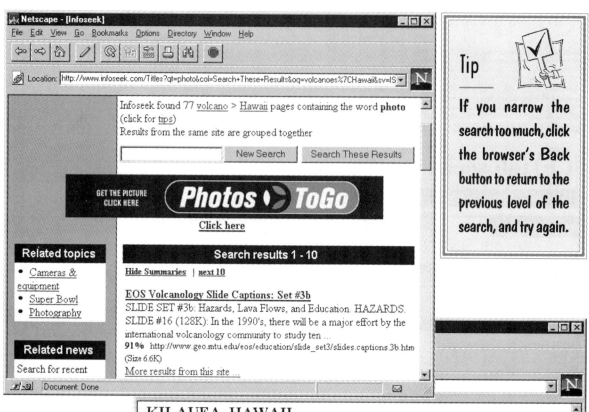

Tip

If you narrow the search too much, click the browser's Back button to return to the previous level of the search, and try again.

After three levels of searches, I'm down to 77 hits – almost all highly relevant – and I found some great photos at a site on the top page.

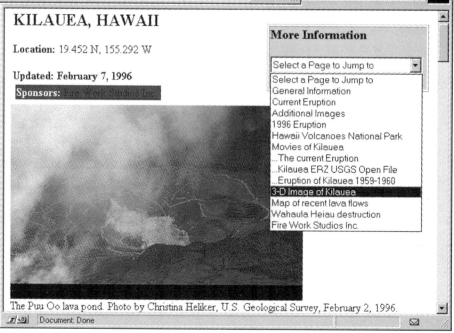

Basic steps

1 Go to Magellan at:
http://www.mckinley.com

2 Enter your search word(s) or expression.

3 Select the area to search – Reviewed sites, Green light sites or the entire Web.

4 Click **search** .

5 Scroll through and view the results or click **find similar** to get more pages on the same topic.

Take note

Magellan also has organised its reviewed and Green light sites into a subject-based catalog.

Magellan has two unique features. First, it has a database of **Green light** sites – sites that have been reviewed and found suitable for children. (It also has a database of 60,00 reviewed and 50 million unreviewed sites.)

The second feature is **concept-based searching**. As the search engine travels the Web building its index, it reads documents and learns which words and ideas are associated with one another. So, if you search for 'movies', it will also look for 'video', 'films', 'cinema' and similar.

Search expressions

With a simple list of words, Magellan will look for pages containing any of them, but put those that contain all – or most – at the top of the results list.

● You can use the operators AND, OR and AND NOT to link words. These must be written in CAPITALS.

● The + and – modifiers can be used to insist that words are present or absent from a page.

Find similar

If your keywords have several meanings, the initial results display may cover a range of topics. To focus on the ones you want, read through to find the most suitable result and click on its **find similar**. This is the concept-based searching in action! In the example, the search on 'amazon' found material on the river in Brazil, as well as stuff on parrots, the bookshop, sushi (!) and other irrelevancies. (And if it hadn't been restricted to Green light sites, it would also have found feminist and girlie pages.) The **find similar** link by the Amazon home page turned up a wealth of material on the river basin – the object of the search.

①　Go to Magellan

②　Enter search words

④　Search

③　Set the area

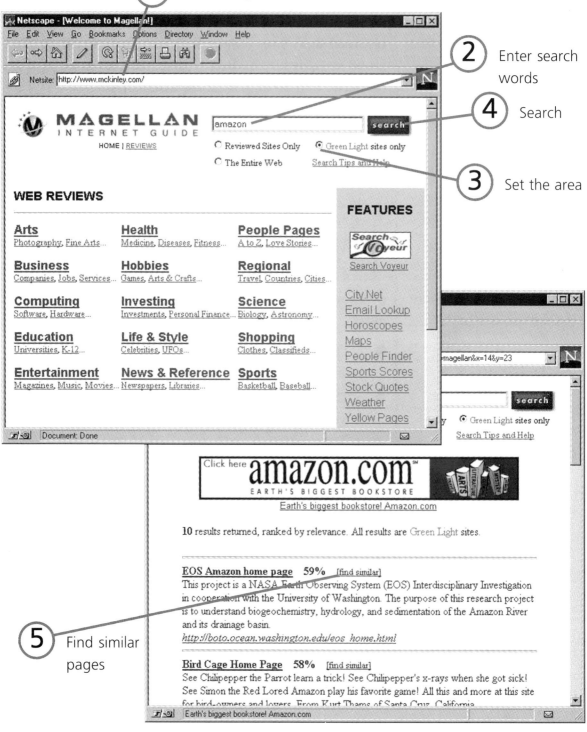

⑤　Find similar pages

Basic steps

1 Go to WebCrawler at:
http://webcrawler.com

2 Enter the search word(s) or expression.

3 Click Search .

4 If the URLs alone don't tell you enough about the finds, get more detail by clicking **summaries**.

Tip

If you can't find any useful material, there is a Try this search at Excite option at the end of the results page.

WebCrawler has a database of around 2 million sites, with full-text indexing of all the pages at these sites.

A simple search checks for any matching word, but lists first those that match all words. There is no check for alternative endings, except for plurals. If you want to search for an exact phrase, enclose it in quotes.

The normal AND, OR and NOT logical operators can be used – in upper or lower case – and with brackets( )around parts of complex expressions.

WebCrawler also supports NEAR and ADJ.

● NEAR, by itself, specifies that the linked words must be adjacent to each other in either order.

● NEAR followed by a slash and a number specifies that the linked words must be within so may words of each other, in either order. For example, to find a page containing 'Java programming' or 'programming in Java', you would search for:

> programming NEAR/3 Java

● ADJ specifies that the linked words must be adjacent and in the order given. This is almost the same as searching for an exact phrase, except that plurals would also be matched.

Take note

You can also reach WebCrawler from the results pages of searches at its sister site, Magellan.

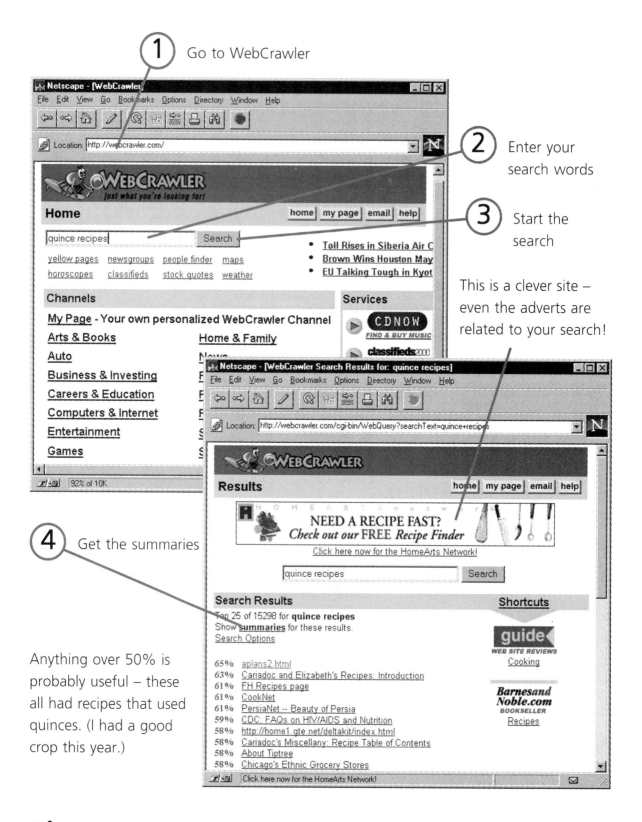

① Go to WebCrawler

② Enter your search words

③ Start the search

This is a clever site – even the adverts are related to your search!

④ Get the summaries

Anything over 50% is probably useful – these all had recipes that used quinces. (I had a good crop this year.)

56

In the example screenshot, the search for 'quince recipes' has been passed to Excite from WebCrawler.

Magellan, WebCrawler and Excite, though separate sites, are closely linked. Excite has the largest database of the three, so if a search at Magellan or WebCrawler fails to come up trumps, try here – you can pass a query directly from one of the others to Excite.

You can go directly to Excite at:

http://www.excite.com

If you start a new search at Excite, write your search expression in the same way as at Magellan.

A search can be refined by selecting keywords – Excite draws these from the hits on the results page.

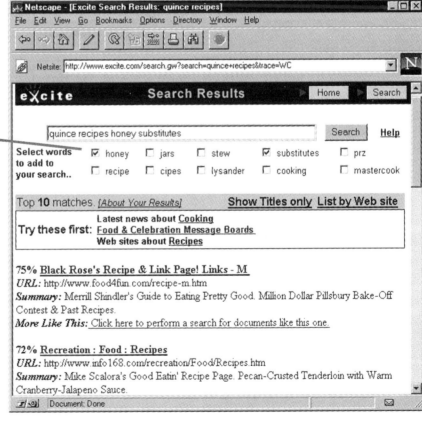

Tip

Excite does the same concept-based searching as Magellan.

Open Text

Open Text also has a full text index, but this is to over 5 million sites – and many millions of documents. Its database has FTP and gopher files, as well as the Web pages, and it is multilingual – including non-European character sets.

With a simple search, your only option is the match style – all the words, any of the words or the exact phrase.

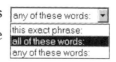

The Power Search has two sets of options, which can be applied to up to 5 words or phrases.

You can select where to look in a file – in its **Title**, **Summary**, **First Heading**, **URL** or **Anywhere**. The **Hyperlink** option is used to find pages that link to a given URL.

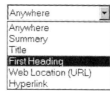

The words can be linked with the operators **And**, **Or**, **But not**, **Near** (within 80 characters) or **Followed by** (within 80 characters).

❑ **Simple Search**

1 Go to Open Text at:
http://www.opentext.com

2 Select the match style.

3 Enter the keywords.

4 Click Search .

5 If you do not find what you want, click **improve your search**.

6 Set where to look for each word.

7 Set the operator to link each word to the next.

8 Click Search .

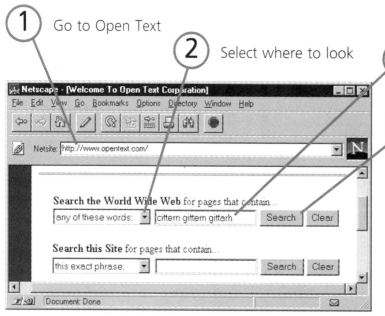

① Go to Open Text

② Select where to look

③ Enter the search words

④ Click Search

Take note

An Open Text search does not check for plurals or other endings.

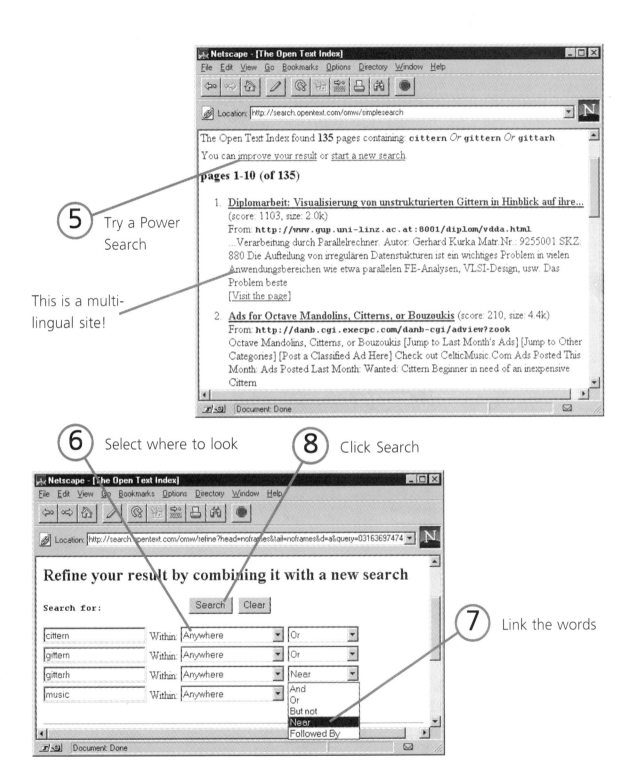

⑤ Try a Power Search

This is a multi-lingual site!

Netscape - [The Open Text Index]

File Edit View Go Bookmarks Options Directory Window Help

Location: http://search.opentext.com/omw/simplesearch

The Open Text Index found **135** pages containing: `cittern` *Or* `gittern` *Or* `gittarh`

You can improve your result or start a new search.

pages 1-10 (of 135)

1. Diplomarbeit: Visualisierung von unstrukturierten Gittern in Hinblick auf ihre...
   (score: 1103, size: 2.0k)
   From: `http://www.gup.uni-linz.ac.at:8001/diplom/vdda.html`
   ...Verarbeitung durch Parallelrechner. Autor: Gerhard Kurka Matr.Nr.: 9255001 SKZ:
   880 Die Aufteilung von irregulären Datenstukturen ist ein wichtiges Problem in vielen
   Anwendungsbereichen wie etwa parallelen FE-Analysen, VLSI-Design, usw. Das
   Problem beste
   [Visit the page]

2. Ads for Octave Mandolins, Citterns, or Bouzoukis (score: 210, size: 4.4k)
   From: `http://danb.cgi.execpc.com/danb-cgi/adview?zook`
   Octave Mandolins, Citterns, or Bouzoukis [Jump to Last Month's Ads] [Jump to Other
   Categories] [Post a Classified Ad Here] Check out CelticMusic.Com Ads Posted This
   Month: Ads Posted Last Month: Wanted: Cittern Beginner in need of an inexpensive
   Cittern

Document: Done

⑥ Select where to look

⑧ Click Search

Netscape - [The Open Text Index]

File Edit View Go Bookmarks Options Directory Window Help

Location: http://search.opentext.com/omw/refine?head=noframes&tail=noframes&d=a&query=03163697474

Refine your result by combining it with a new search

Search for:

[Search] [Clear]

⑦ Link the words

cittern	Within: Anywhere	Or
gittern	Within: Anywhere	Or
gittarh	Within: Anywhere	Near
music	Within: Anywhere	

And
Or
But not
Near
Followed By

Document: Done

59

The Electric Library

This is a searchable database, rather than a search engine. Its links are primarily to resources within the Electric Library site, though it also has external links. Unlike all the services we have looked at so far, this is not free. If you want to use the Electric Library, it will cost you $60 a year. It is worth noting for two reasons:

● it does offer a huge amount of quality information;

● it may well be a pointer to the future – expect to see an increasing number of sites charging for access to their information.

Basic steps

1 Go to the Electric Library at:
http://www.elibrary.com

2 Enter your keyword(s) – no operators.

3 Select the sources.

4 Drop down the **Subjects** list and select one if appropriate.

5 Click Go!.

6 Select a document.

1 Go to the Electric Library

2 Enter keywords

5 Click Go!

3 Set the sources

4 Pick a subject area?

The documents in the main list are all within the Electric Library. If the search finds external links, they are listed lower down on the page.

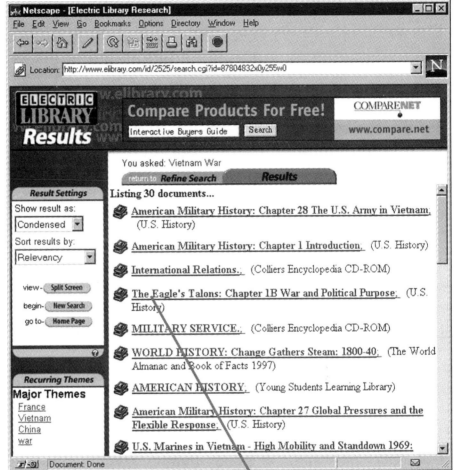

⑥ Read a document

Take note

The Electric Library is quite different from anything else in this chapter. I have included it at this point because it had to go somewhere, and it fits better here than anywhere else in the book!

Tip

Save long documents as files and read them off-line – it's cheaper!

Summary

❏ **Simple searches** – just using keywords – are handled in almost the same way by all search engines. Most also accept the AND, OR and NOT **logical operators**, and the +/– **modifiers**.

❏ At **AltaVista** you can keep the returns down to a reasonable level by refining the search, using the Way Cool topics map, or specifying an advanced search.

❏ **HotBot** has indexed almost all the Web, but its option-based search form makes it easy to focus a search.

❏ **Lycos** offers a good full-Web search, and is an excellent place to look for pictures and sounds.

❏ At **InfoSeek** you can narrow a search down in stages, searching within a set of results for a new keyword.

❏ **Magellan's Green light** sites make this a prime site for children to use – but it also has reviewed sites across the full range of topics, and links to most of the Web.

❏ The **WebCrawler** searches both the title and the full text of over 2 million Web sites.

❏ If searches at Magellan or WebCrawler fail, you can pass the search across to the sister site, **Excite**, which has a far larger database.

❏ **Open Text** has a full text index of over 5 million sites, with FTP and gopher files as well as Web documents. It is probably the best site for multilingual use.

❏ The **Electric Library** is a good research resource, but charges for access to its database.

4 Searching the UK

UK directory

If you want to find local suppliers, clubs, courses, the main Internet directories and search engines may not be the best place to look – simply because you will get too many irrelevant links. If you want local stuff, look in a local directory. In the UK, the first place to try is UK directory. It has links to UK businesses, shops, schools, colleges and government organisations, news, travel, entertainment and other services.

Unless you are looking for something very specific it is probably simplest to work your way through the well organised catalog. If you do need to search, use the Full Search routine for better control.

Basic steps

1 Go to UK directory at:
http://www.ukdirectory.co.uk

2 Browse through the catalog.

or

3 Click on **Full Search**.

4 Enter the search words.

5 Set the match to **ANY** or **ALL** words.

6 Enter any words to **Exclude**, if appropriate.

7 Click ➡ **GO!**

if you get too many hits...

8 Click on a keyword to narrow the search.

(1) Go to UK directory

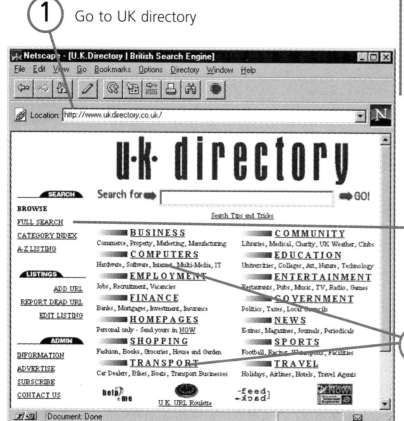

(3) Click Full Search

(2) Browse the catalog

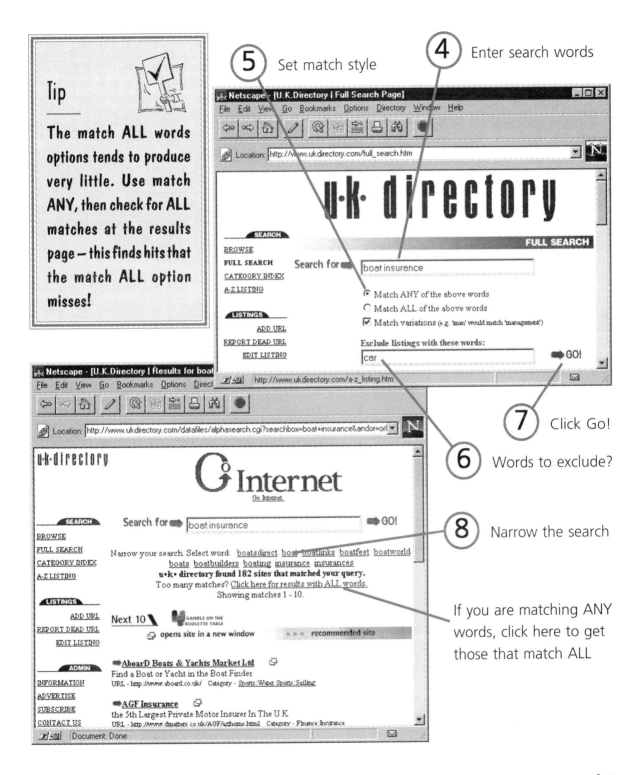

⑤ Set match style

④ Enter search words

⑦ Click Go!

⑥ Words to exclude?

⑧ Narrow the search

If you are matching ANY words, click here to get those that match ALL

UK Index

The UK Index is a good source of links to suppliers and other commercial organisations, though not so good for non-commercial information.

Searches only operate on their own entries – not on UK Web sites and pages in general – but are simple to set up. The organisation of their entries by category makes it very easy to focus a search.

Basic steps

1 Go to UK Index at:
http://www.ukindex.co.uk

2 Enter up to two separate words or a single phrase.

3 Select **And, Or** or **Phrase**.

4 Select the categories to be searched.

5 Click Submit .

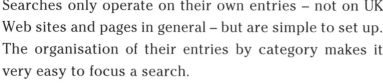

① Go to UK Index

② Enter search words

③ Set the match style

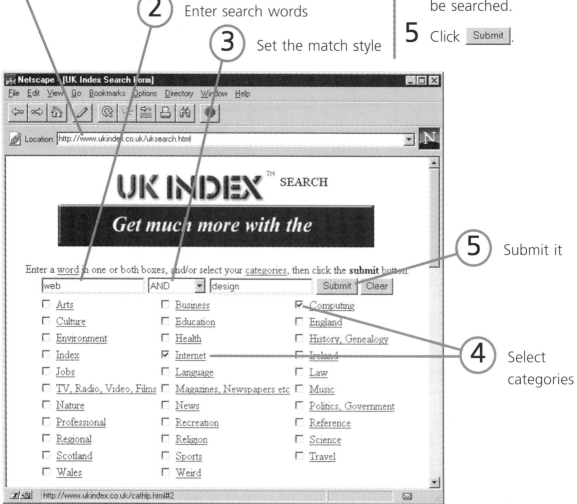

⑤ Submit it

④ Select categories

Basic steps

1 Go to UK Search at:
http://www.uksearch.com

2 Enter your keywords.

3 Select where to look.

4 Define the results display.

5 Click Search .

The UK Search database holds links to something over 250,000 UK sites, which must represent a high proportion of the total number.

The search options are limited. You can choose whether to look in the title, heading, text or all of each document. You can also set the style and number of the results display. When searching, it will try to match any of the words, but list first those that contain all of them. Logical operators and other search modifiers do not work here.

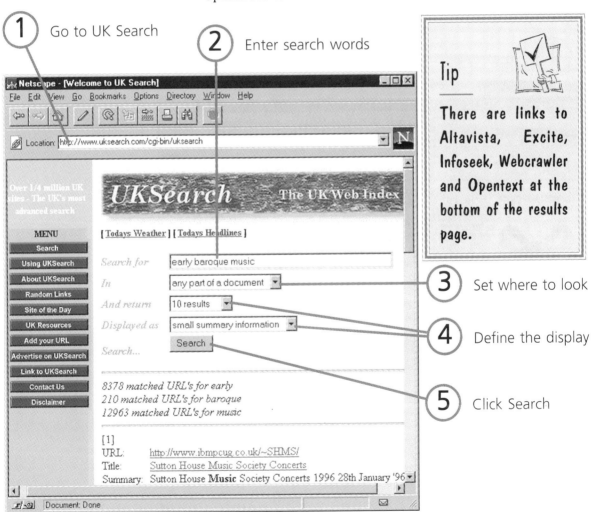

① Go to UK Search

② Enter search words

③ Set where to look

④ Define the display

⑤ Click Search

Tip

There are links to Altavista, Excite, Infoseek, Webcrawler and Opentext at the bottom of the results page.

Yell

Yell is more than just a directory. It is also the home of electronic Yellow Pages – with links to Scoot – and hosts a comprehensive Film Finder, and a good London Guide.

It's a bright, jolly site, heavy on graphics, though it has such good telephone/modem links (well, it is run by BT!) that it pages download very quickly.

The directory to UK sites, and its search facilities, are in the Yellow Web.

1 Go to Yell at:
http://www.yell.co.uk

❑ **Searching**

2 Click on Yellow Web.

3 Select a heading and browse the catalogue.

or

4 Enter the search words.

5 Select the match style.

6 Click Search

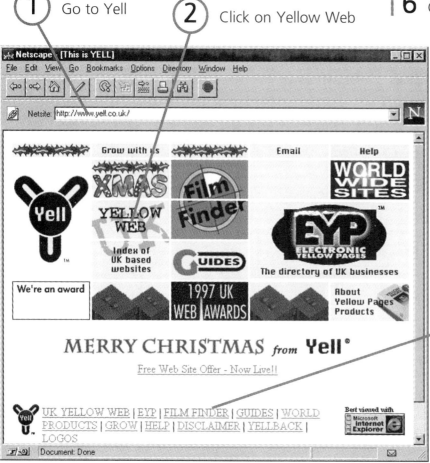

① Go to Yell

② Click on Yellow Web

You can also navigate around the site using the main page titles – these are on the bottom of every page.

Searching at Yellow Web

This is another bare-bones search routine. You can only enter plain words – no operators or +/– symbols. The only real control is over the match style, and the options here are unusual. You can match all the words in the given order, or in any order, or match one or more words, or the words within other words (i.e. 'foot' also finds 'bigfoot' and 'football').

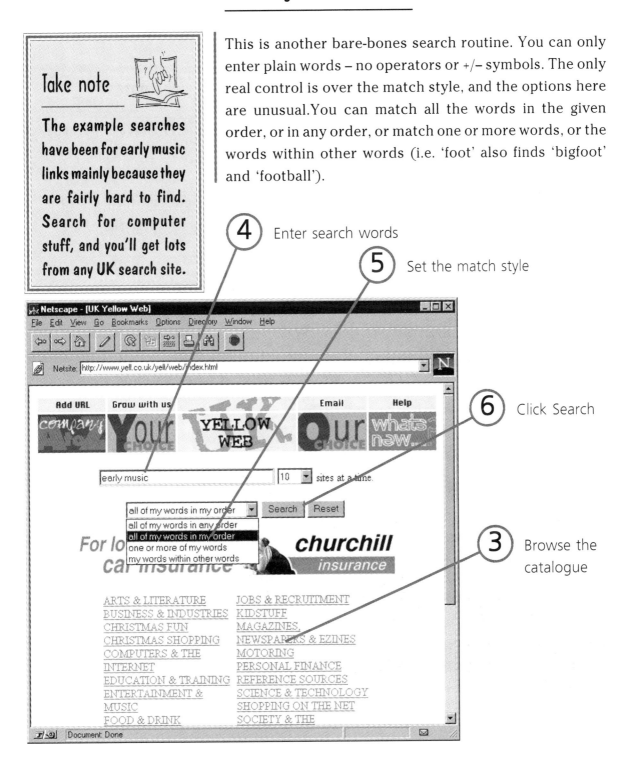

④ Enter search words

⑤ Set the match style

⑥ Click Search

③ Browse the catalogue

Yell for more!

EYP – Electronic Yellow Pages – contain the full UK set of classified phone books in a searchable database. The trickiest part to using this is getting right term for the Business Type. You can take a guess at this, and if it doesn't match any of the set Type names, EYP will suggest some possibilities. Alternatively, you can look through the A-Z of Business Types and pick a term from there – it takes a few moments for the lists to load (they are long) – but when you pick a Type, the system returns you to the search page, with the term in place.

Take note

EYP gives you the names, addresses and phone numbers of businesses – but not their e-mail or Web page addresses.

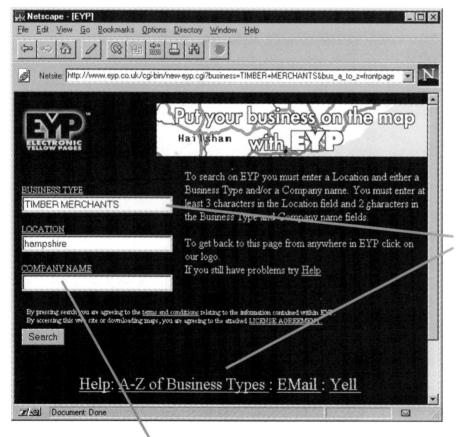

Use the A-Z of Business Types if you have trouble finding the right term for the Type.

You can also search for companies by name

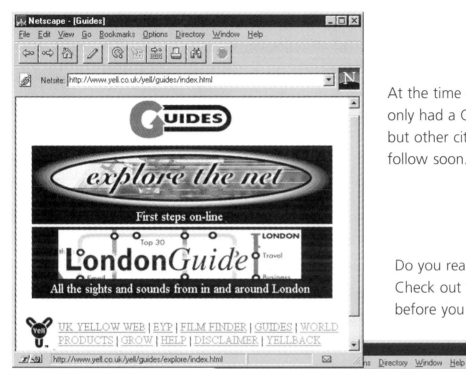

At the time of writing, Yell only had a Guide to London, but other city guides should follow soon.

Do you really want to see it? Check out the summaries before you go.

At the next stage, you pick the town and/or film title, so you can either find what's on locally, or where you will have to go to see a particular film.

Summary

❑ If you are looking for **local firms and organisations**, you are probably better off using a search engine or directory that is based in your own country.

❑ **UK directory** has a comprehensive catalogue of UK sites which you can access pages through its menu system or its search facility.

❑ When searching at the **UK Index** you specify which categories to search through – a simple and effective way to focus a search.

❑ **UK Search** has probably the largest database of UK sites, and if you need to extend a search globally, it has links to several major search engines.

❑ **Yell** hosts the **Electronic Yellow Pages,** as well as a UK Web search engine and other facilities.

Take note

I've concentrated on the UK, because that is where I live and where I expect most readers will live, but if live elsewhere, you should be able to find your local directories and search engines by heading to Yahoo, and looking up your country in its Regional menu.

5 One-stop searches

All-in-One Search page

There are many organisations and home pages run by enthusiasts that offer a 'one-stop' approach to searching. The style varies. Some will take your search words and pass them to a set of engines, then present you with all the results. These are easy to use, but limit you to simple searches. Others have entry forms for many engines, but you have to perform each search separately. This is more trouble, but allow you to write more complex search expressions geared to each engine. The All-in-One Search page takes the latter approach – and it doesn't just link to the standard search engines. You can also hunt for files, people, documents and other resources from here.

Basic steps

1 Go to All-in-One at:
**http:www/albany.net/
allinone**

2 Select a set – use the
World Wide Web for
general work.

3 Select a search engine.

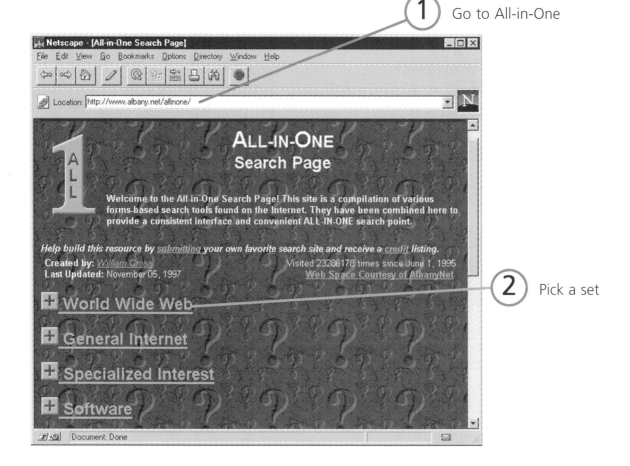

Go to All-in-One

Pick a set

4 Enter your keywords, using logical operators and +/– symbols if appropriate.

5 Click Search .

3 Select an engine

4 Type your search words or expression

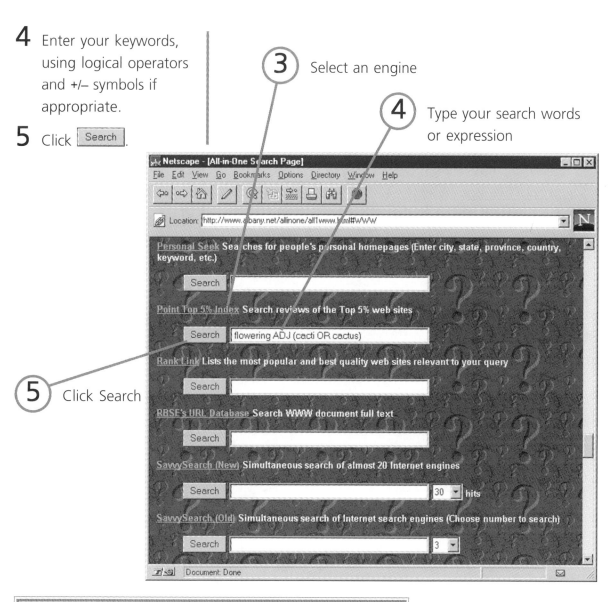

5 Click Search

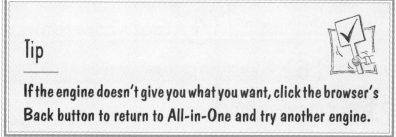

Tip

If the engine doesn't give you what you want, click the browser's Back button to return to All-in-One and try another engine.

Savvy Search

Savvy Search is a service run by Colorado State University. It takes your keywords and passes them to a set of three engines (which three depends upon the nature of your search). The results can be listed by engine, or integrated – integration takes a little longer, but eliminates duplicates.

1 Go to:
http://guaraldi.cs.
colostate.edu:2000/
and select **Savvy Search**.

2 Enter your keywords.

3 Select the types of information you want.

4 Select the match style – **all** terms, **any** terms or the **exact phrase**.

5 Set the number of results from each site.

6 Select a display format.

7 Turn on **Integrate results**, if wanted.

8 Click [SavvySearch!].

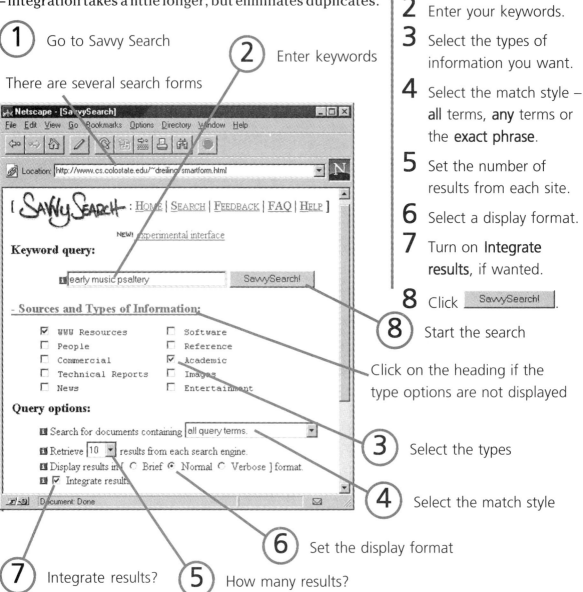

(1) Go to Savvy Search

There are several search forms

(2) Enter keywords

(8) Start the search

Click on the heading if the type options are not displayed

(3) Select the types

(4) Select the match style

(6) Set the display format

(7) Integrate results?

(5) How many results?

76

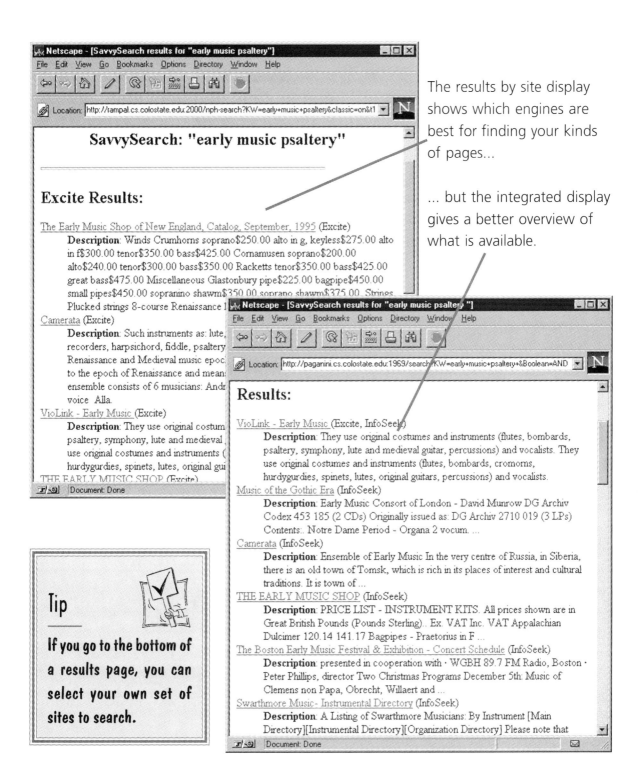

The results by site display shows which engines are best for finding your kinds of pages...

... but the integrated display gives a better overview of what is available.

Tip

If you go to the bottom of a results page, you can select your own set of sites to search.

MetaCrawler

MetaCrawler, like Savvy Search, runs the searches for you, though it searches through the same ten engines, while Savvy Search checks three at a time.

The basic search form is similar, but with fewer options, and the results are always integrated before display.

The Power Search allows you to set which continent to search, how long to wait at each search engine before calling Timeout, and the number of results per page and per source. It does not give you any more control over the search expression.

1 Go to MetaCrawler at:
http:// www.metacrawler.com

2 Enter your keywords.

3 Select where to search.

4 Select the match style – **all**, **any** or **exact phrase**.

5 Click ⬚ Search ⬚.

6 If you want to change the number of hits, or the time to wait for an engine to respond, select **Power Search**.

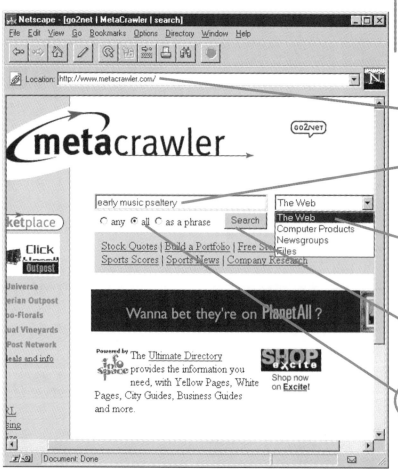

1. Go to MetaCrawler
2. Enter the search words
3. Set the search area
5. Start the search
4. Set the match style

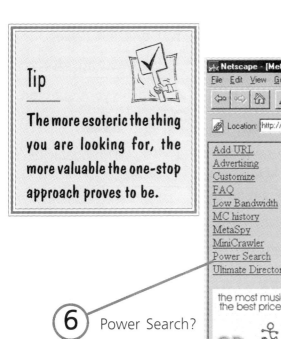

6 Power Search?

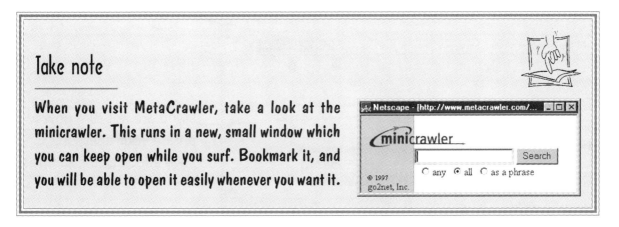

Ask Jeeves

Ask Jeeves is a mixture of marketing organisation and search site. Ask a question here, and – if Jeeves does not have the answer at his fingertips – he will pass it on to half a dozen or so search engines and show you what they find.

The sort of questions that Jeeves can answer directly are of the 'where can I buy...' type, as companies advertise their wares there – the organisation also markets some goods itself. And the answers to these questions tend to be more relevant to US surfers.

Whatever the question, ask it in ordinary English – but be ready to ask it more than once, and in different ways as Jeeves may not quite get your drift the first time.

Basic steps

1 Go to Ask Jeeves at:

http://www.askjeeves.com

2 Type in your question.

3 Click **Ask**.

❑ You will probably be offered several rephrased questions.

4 Pick from the drop-down list by the question that is closest to what you mean.

5 Click **Ask** again.

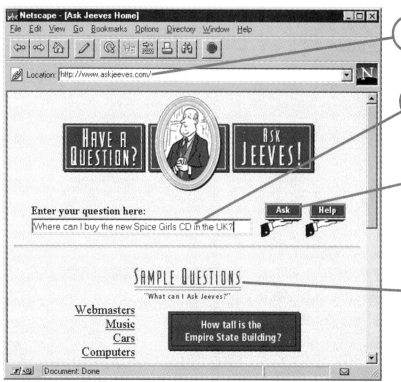

① Go to Ask Jeeves

② Type your question

③ Click Ask

If you are not sure how to phrase your questions, have a look at the samples.

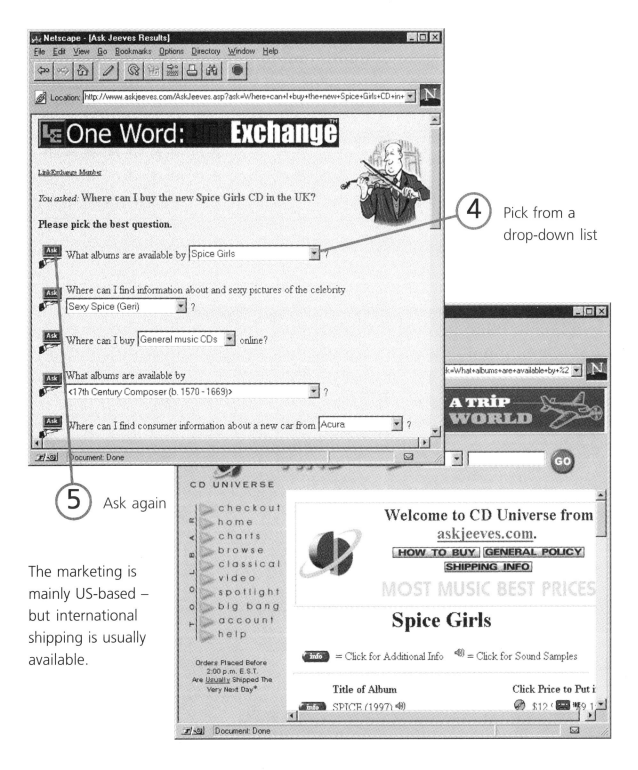

④ Pick from a drop-down list

⑤ Ask again

The marketing is mainly US-based – but international shipping is usually available.

Ask the right question

You have to ask the right question to get the right answer, but what is right? Trial and error will lead you to the correct phrasing, but making sure that the question contains the right keywords will help.

For example, I asked this question 'How can I arrange a holiday in Vienna?' The answer is shown below – Jeeves focused on 'holiday' and produced little of any use, though AltaVista picked up a few possible links.

On the opposite page, you can see the results from 'Travel and hotels in Vienna' – it's not a proper question, but it has the words to stimulate the right answers.

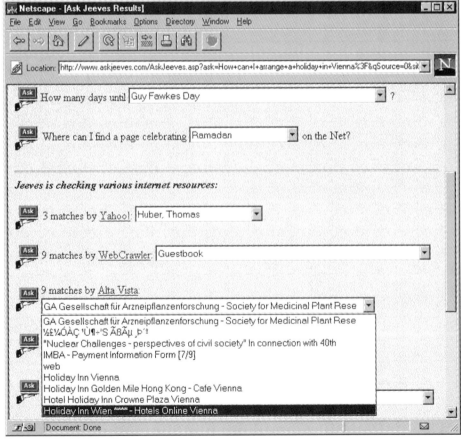

Results from other search engines are listed below the set of Jeeves questions. In this example, it seems that Jeeves passed on the words 'holidays' and 'Vienna' – and got very mixed results!

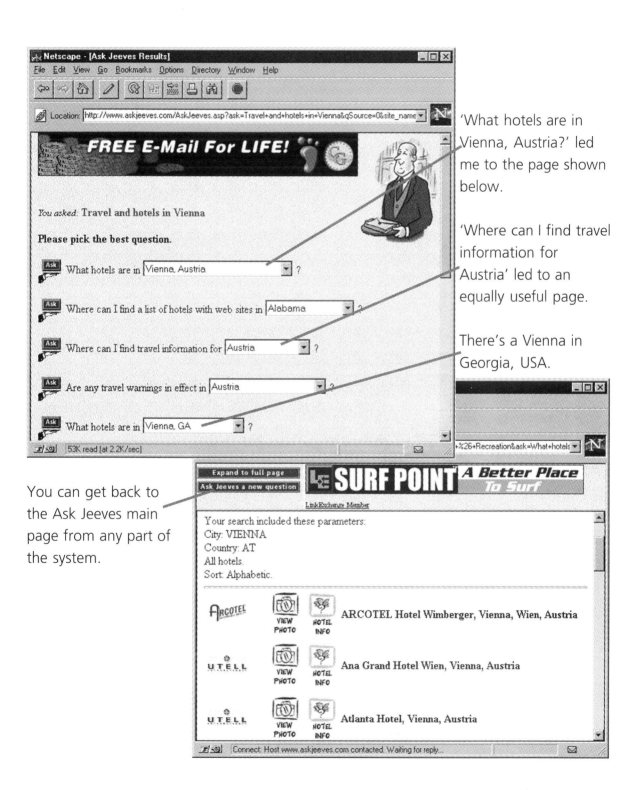

'What hotels are in Vienna, Austria?' led me to the page shown below.

'Where can I find travel information for Austria' led to an equally useful page.

There's a Vienna in Georgia, USA.

You can get back to the Ask Jeeves main page from any part of the system.

Netscape Search

Netscape users have easy access to five of the best search sites, with links to a couple of dozen more through the Internet Search option on the Directory menu (on the Edit menu in Communicator). This links to the search page at Netscape's home site. You can set up simple searches, or select a catalog heading from here, and are then transferred to the search site for the results.

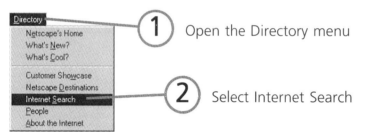

(1) Open the Directory menu

(2) Select Internet Search

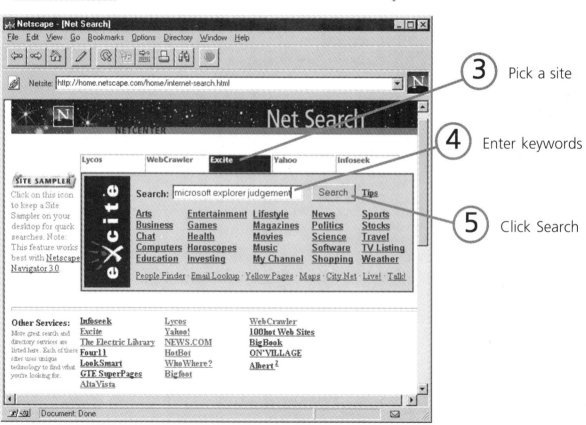

(3) Pick a site

(4) Enter keywords

(5) Click Search

Basic steps

1 Go to the **Internet Search** page.

2 Select your search site.

3 Click 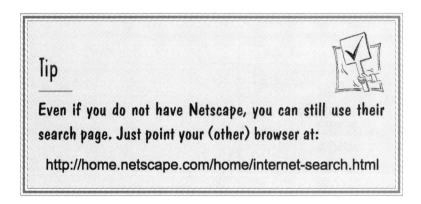.

4 The new window will be larger than the sample panel – adjust it down to size.

5 Run your searches as normal.

6 When you are finished, click the Close button to exit the window.

The Site Sampler

If you want to search for a number of different items or browse the catalogue at a search site, you can open the Site Sampler search panel in a separate window. It will then stay open while the main window displays the data from the search site.

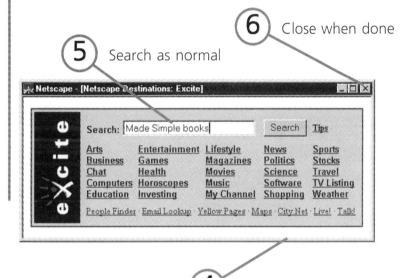

(6) Close when done

(5) Search as normal

(4) Adjust the window size

Tip

Even if you do not have Netscape, you can still use their search page. Just point your (other) browser at:

http://home.netscape.com/home/internet-search.html

IE Exploring

With Internet Explorer 4.0, Microsoft has introduced a screen layout that is very convenient for searching. Searches are run in the left-hand panel, and the results are displayed and found pages are viewed in the main panel. If you want to see more of a page, the search panel can be closed with a click of a button, then re-opened later with its contents still in place.

Basic steps

1 Open the **Help** menu, point to **Microsoft on the Web** and choose **Search the Web**.

or

2 Click .

3 Type the search words.

4 Select a search engine.

5 Click **Search**.

Select Help – Microsoft on the Web – Search the Web

Take note

This search technique can only be used with Internet Explorer. Microsoft do offer an 'All-in-One' search page for use by other browsers, but it has a different style. To try it, go to:

http://www.microsoft.com/access/allinone.asp

③ Enter your search words

② Click Search

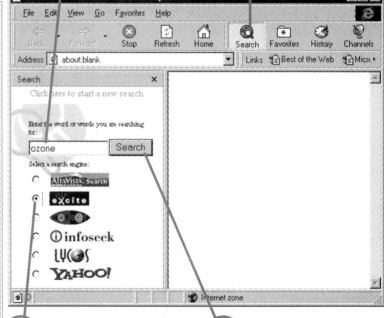

④ Select an engine

⑤ Start the search

Click here to return to the initial search panel, with its set of search engines

You can run more searches or refine your existing one, at the same engine

Toggle the search panel display on and off by clicking the Search button

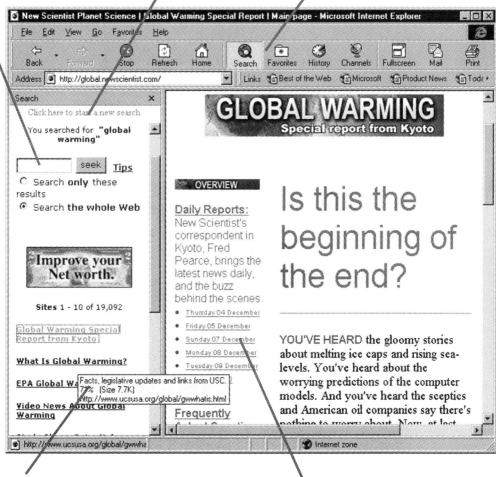

Only links are displayed, but if you want to know more about a hit, point to it and wait for the pop-up panel to give you any other available information

If you follow up links, the new pages will be displayed in this panel, without affecting the search panel

Summary

❑ If you want to search for a lot of material, or expect to have trouble finding something, the one-stop approach will give you easier access to a number of search engines.

❑ The All-in-One Search page has links to over 120 search engines and other specialized search facilities.

❑ Savvy Search will pass your query to a set of three engines and display the results from them all.

❑ MetaCrawler will run your search through up to ten of the top search engines, and integrate the results before display.

❑ The minicrawler runs in a separate window, making it simpler to perform a series of searches and view the results.

❑ At Ask Jeeves, you can ask natural language questions when performing a search. It is a good place to look for products and services, but will also run searches for other information on a range of engines.

❑ Netscape's Search page has links to the best search engines and sites. Its Site Sample can be run in a separate window for more convenient searching.

❑ The Internet Explorer 4.0 two-panel screen allows you to search and view results at the same time.

6 Finding files

Software at c|net

Basic steps

Amongst c|net's many activities, it runs **Software Central** – a great place to find freeware, shareware and commercial software for PCs or Macintosh computers.

The simplest way to find software is to work through the catalog. The categories are well organised, with the first jump taking you to the program listings. These show the dates and the number of times it has been downloaded – a reasonable indicator of its quality. Some listings are very lengthy, though sorting by downloads should bring the best to the top. When you select a program, you are taken to a page showing a longer description, its size, price, etc. You can download from there with a click.

1 Go to: **http://www.cnet.com** and select **Software Central** from its top page.

2 Select a **Category**.

3 Click on a likely program.

4 Click to download.

Or

5 Go back and look at another.

1 Go to Software Central at www.cnet.com

The Quick Search is good if you know the name of the program you want – otherwise it is simpler to look in a suitable Category

2 Select a Category

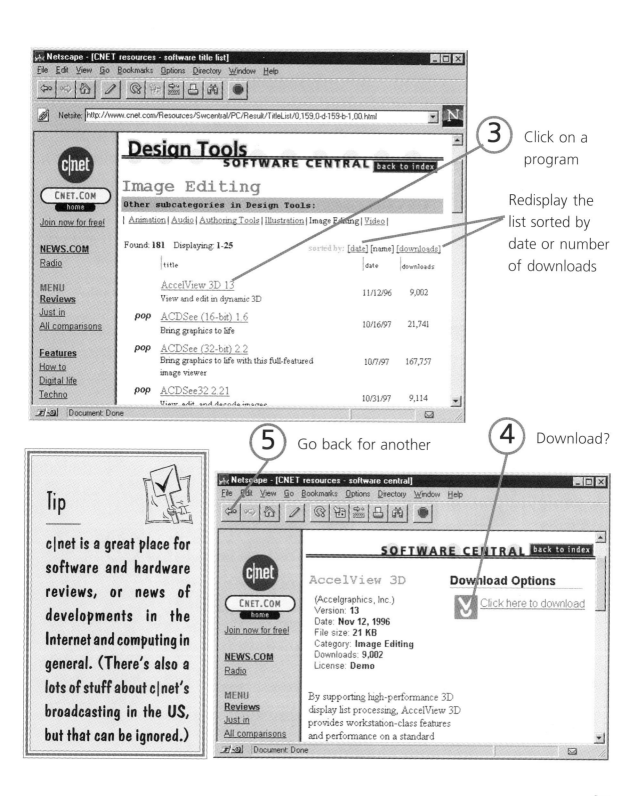

③ Click on a program

Redisplay the list sorted by date or number of downloads

⑤ Go back for another

④ Download?

shareware.com

Another valuable c|net service is **shareware.com.** It has literally megabytes of shareware (and freeware) programs. This is a place for searching, not browsing!

The Search routine looks for a match in the names and in the descriptions of the programs.

● If you are just starting to build your shareware collection, try the Most Popular selection.

1 Go to: http:// www.shareware.com

2 In the **Quick Search** box type the name or a key descriptive word.

3 Select your operating system.

4 Click **Search** and wait.

5 Read the descriptions to find the right file.

① Go to shareware.com

② Type the name or a keyword

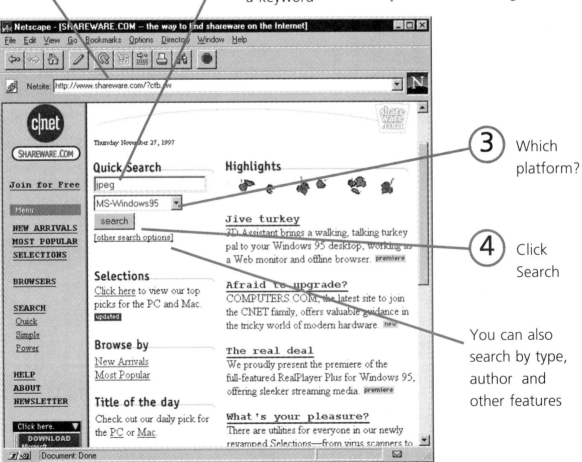

③ Which platform?

④ Click Search

You can also search by type, author and other features

92

6 Click on the filename to start the download – saving the file as usual.

6 Click to download

5 Read about the files

Check the size – is it worth the download time? This would take 10 to 15 minutes to download.

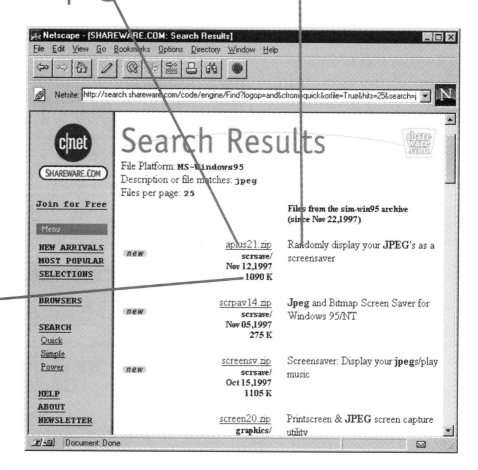

Take note

c|net has more software at
http://www.gamecenter.com
and
http:// www.download.com

Tip

To be kept informed of new arrivals, click **Newsletter** and get on the list for Shareware Dispatch, their e-mail newsletter.

Shareware at Jumbo

Jumbo started up in mid-1995, with the aim of becoming the biggest and best shareware site on the Net. By late 1997, it had around 200,000 files at the tip of its trunk – and growing by nearly 10,000 a month. Despite this rate of growth, the files were well organised, though some links were incorrect or inactive.

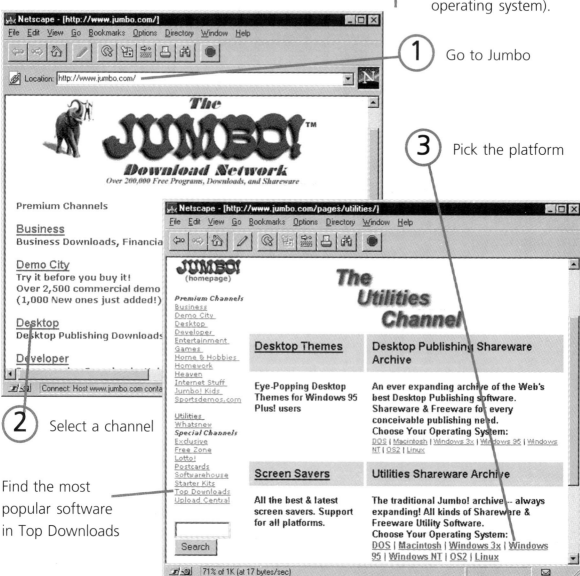

Go to Jumbo

Pick the platform

Select a channel

Find the most popular software in Top Downloads

4 Select a category.

5 Scroll through the list – click  to find out more about the file.

6 Click 🐘 to download and pick a site – try the closest first.

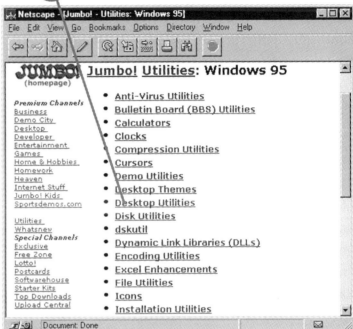

Choose a category

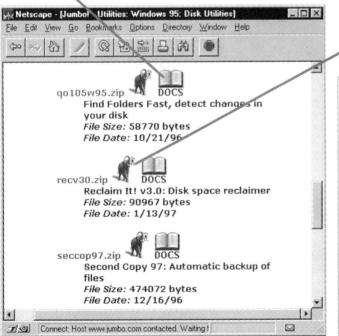

Read all about it

Click to download

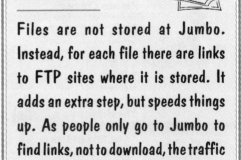

Take note

Files are not stored at Jumbo. Instead, for each file there are links to FTP sites where it is stored. It adds an extra step, but speeds things up. As people only go to Jumbo to find links, not to download, the traffic is lighter than at other software sites.

Other shareware sites

New shareware sites are springing up all the time – and for fairly obvious reasons. It costs nothing, except a little research time, to put shareware links on your page, and shareware pulls in the surfers. Everyone likes to have visitors! And if you are a commercial site, the more visitors you get, the more you can charge for your advertising.

The quality varies, but here are a two of the best.

Tucows

This is an entertaining and useful site, listing vast quantities of reviewed and rated shareware. Though the emphasis is on Winsock applications – i.e. those which are used while you are on-line to the Internet – it also includes HTML and graphics editors and utilities and much more besides. Each is shown with essential details, a review, a rating and – crucially – a link from which it can be downloaded.

1 Go to Tucows at:
   http://www.tucows.com

2 Select your region, then the closest site.

3 Click on the category.

4 Scroll through the list, reading the description and noting the rating.

5 Click **Download** when you find a suitable application.

1 Go to Tucows

Tucows has been so successful that it is now has many 'mirror' sites – places that store the same sets of pages and files. Starting from the home page, find the site closest to you – and bookmark it for future use.

2 Select a region, then a site

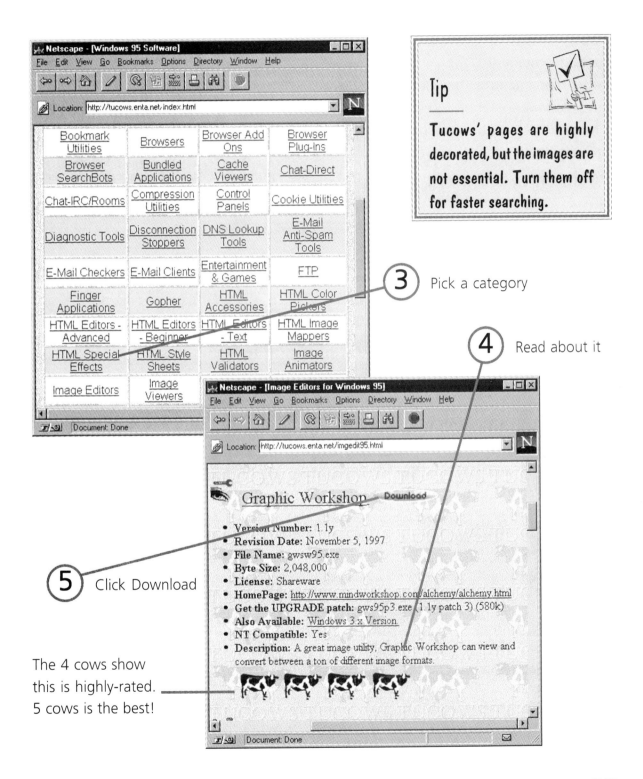

Netscape - [Windows 95 Software]

File Edit View Go Bookmarks Options Directory Window Help

Location: http://tucows.enta.net/index.html

Bookmark Utilities	Browsers	Browser Add Ons	Browser Plug-Ins
Browser SearchBots	Bundled Applications	Cache Viewers	Chat-Direct
Chat-IRC/Rooms	Compression Utilities	Control Panels	Cookie Utilities
Diagnostic Tools	Disconnection Stoppers	DNS Lookup Tools	E-Mail Anti-Spam Tools
E-Mail Checkers	E-Mail Clients	Entertainment & Games	FTP
Finger Applications	Gopher	HTML Accessories	HTML Color Pickers
HTML Editors - Advanced	HTML Editors - Beginner	HTML Editors - Text	HTML Image Mappers
HTML Special Effects	HTML Style Sheets	HTML Validators	Image Animators
Image Editors	Image Viewers		

Document: Done

Tip

Tucows' pages are highly decorated, but the images are not essential. Turn them off for faster searching.

③ Pick a category

④ Read about it

Netscape - [Image Editors for Windows 95]

File Edit View Go Bookmarks Options Directory Window Help

Location: http://tucows.enta.net/imgedit95.html

Graphic Workshop *Download*

- **Version Number:** 1.1y
- **Revision Date:** November 5, 1997
- **File Name:** gwsw95.exe
- **Byte Size:** 2,048,000
- **License:** Shareware
- **HomePage:** http://www.mindworkshop.com/alchemy/alchemy.html
- **Get the UPGRADE patch:** gws95p3.exe (1.1y patch 3) (580k)
- **Also Available:** Windows 3.x Version.
- **NT Compatible:** Yes
- **Description:** A great image utility, Graphic Workshop can view and convert between a ton of different image formats.

Document: Done

⑤ Click Download

The 4 cows show this is highly-rated. 5 cows is the best!

ZD Net Software Library

This is hosted by ZD Net, one of the Internet's great content providers. This specialises in offering quality, rather than quantity, though over a wide area. It's a good place to look for kids' software and animated (or still) images, as well as the usual range of Internet and desktop tools and applications. The Software Library is at:

http://www.hotfiles.com

Take note

ZD Net's main site is at:
http://www.zdnet.com

If you are just browsing – rather than looking for a particular type of application – check out the quality stuff first!

clicked.com

Take note

Clicked is at:

www.clicked.com

This bills itself as an 'on-line superstore' and is included here for two reasons. First it has a Top 20 Shareware Gallery, with selected applications in each of a range of categories – making it a handy place to pick up some good stuff. Secondly, it hosts 'Baby Time', with a wealth of resources for the mother-to-be and young babies. Which just goes to prove that the Internet is not only for nerds!

To go straight to the Top 20 Shareware, jump to: http://www.clicked.com/ shareware/index.html

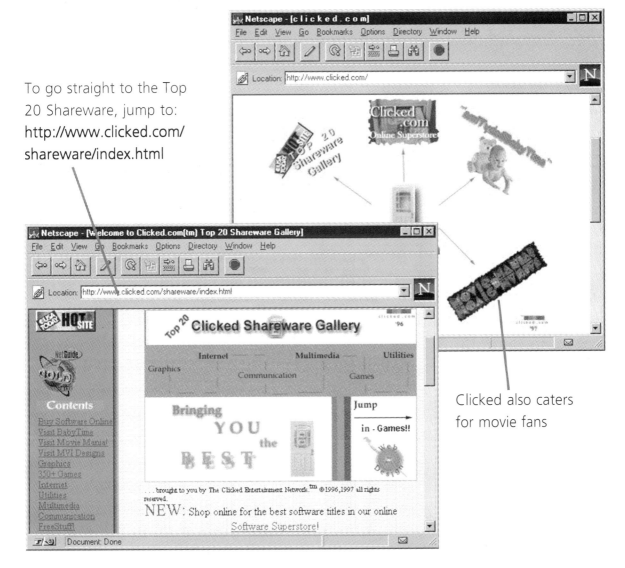

Clicked also caters for movie fans

Browsing the FTP sites

As you surf the Web with your browser, you may come across files that you would like to download. This can be done directly from within the browser. You can even browse through the directories at FTP sites and download from there – though this is done more efficiently with dedicated FTP software.

To find FTP sites from the Web, go to Yahoo and select *Computers and Internet – Internet – FTP sites*.

❑ **Browsing ftp sites**

1 Click on a <u>link</u> to get to a site or go to its URL: **http://***ftpsitename*

2 Enter a **directory** by clicking on its name.

3 When you find a file you want, click on it.

❑ If the browser has a suitable viewer, it will display the file. It can then be saved with **File – Save As** if wanted.

FTP icons

🔙 Parent directory – up one level

📁 Subdirectory

📄 Text – may be formatted

📦 Compressed – usually ZIP for PCs

❓ Index or Help file

Go an FTP site

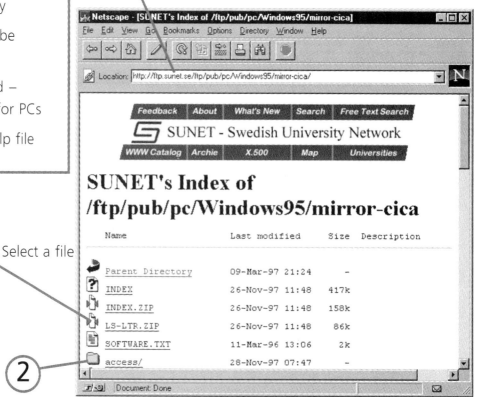

③ Select a file

Change directory ②

❏ **FTP direct**

4 If you have the file's URL, you can jump straight to it with:
ftp://*site/path/filename*

❏ **Downloading**

5 If the browser cannot display the file, it may go to the **Save As** dialog, or display the **Unknown File Type** dialog. Click [S̲ave File...]

6 At the **Save As** dialog, select a folder.

7 The filename will be there already. Change it if it conflicts with an existing filename.

8 Click [S̲ave] and wait while it downloads.

Tip

With large files, at busy times, it may be better to write down the URL and come back for it with **WS_FTP**. (See page 104.)

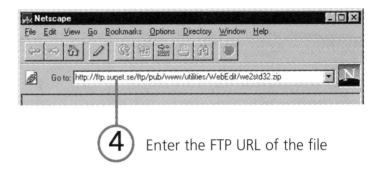

④ Enter the FTP URL of the file

⑤ Save to disk

⑥ Set the directory/folder

⑦ Check the name

⑧ Click save

Hypertext FTP

Some FTP sites now have proper Web pages for simpler access to their files. The big advantage here is that instead of having bare FTP directory listings, you can have an indexed system with descriptions of the files – this can save some wasted downloads!

Oakland University's Software Repository is a good example of an established FTP site that now offers an excellent Web interface. It is mirror of the massive SimTel Coast to Coast Software Repository, hosts some specialist collections, has links to c|net's Virtual Software Library and has its own databanks.

Basic steps

1 Go to Oak at:
http:// www.acs.oakland.edu/ oak/oak.html

2 Select the collection (at Simtel.Net you will have to go down two more levels).

3 Pick a letter to get into the index.

4 Select a category.

5 Browse the files and download as usual.

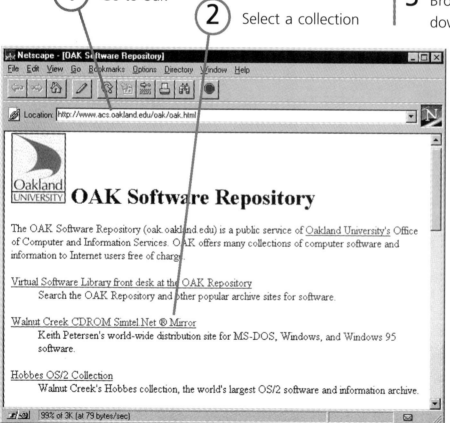

① Go to Oak

② Select a collection

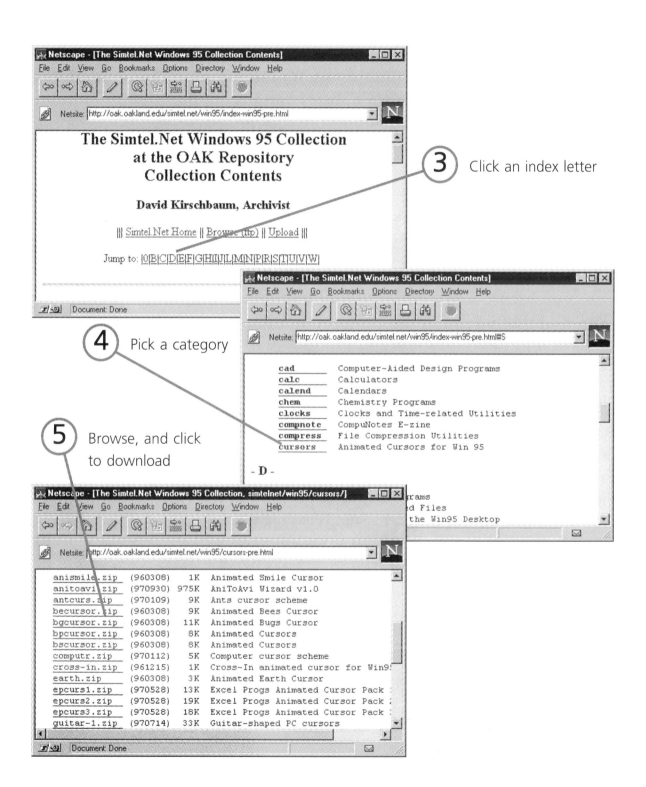

3 Click an index letter

4 Pick a category

5 Browse, and click to download

WS_FTP

If you use the FTP sites a lot, or you want to upload files, you should get some dedicated FTP software. WS_FTP is probably the best of these – and it's free. There are several versions of WS_FTP. The one illustrated here is for Windows 95. Get a copy from the author's (John Junod) home site at:

ftp://ftp2.ipswitch.com/pub/win32

or from any good shareware site. Amongst other places, you'll find it in the Internet section at:

http://www.shareware.com

WS_FTP is a *Winsock compliant* program, which means you must have Winsock running – and be logged on to your service provider before you can use it. If you have Windows 95, Winsock is built into the Dial-Up Networking.

Anonymous login

When connecting to an FTP site, you normally give 'anonymous' as the user name and your e-mail address as the password. This is known as **anonymous login**. The main exception is when you use FTP to upload your home page files to your access provider's site. Then, you will give the same User ID and password that you use when logging in at the start of a normal session.

With WS_FTP, you give your e-mail address during the installation process, so it is in place when needed in setting up a new connection.

Basic steps

1 Go on-line then run WS_FTP.

2 Pick a site from the **Profile** list – there are a dozen already set up.

or

3 Create a profile for a new site. Click
[New] and enter a profile name and the exact **Host name**.

4 If this uses the (normal) anonymous login, tick **Anonymous.**

5 Switch to the **Startup** tab and enter the **Remote Host Directory**, if known.

6 Click [Apply] if you have set up a new profile, or made changes that you want to keep.

7 Click [OK] to start the connection.

Making the connection

WS_FTP is simple enough to use – just tell it where you want to go, and what directory to start at, then send it off to make the connection.

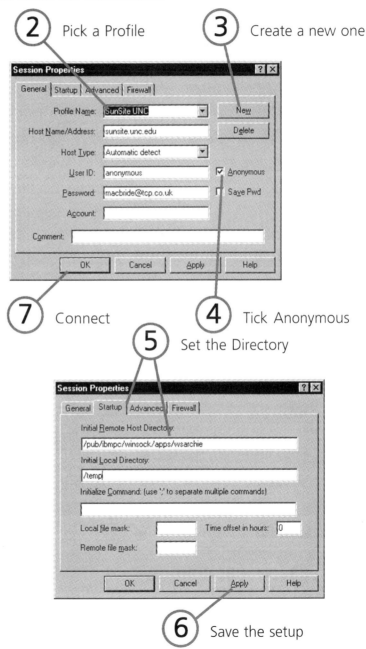

② Pick a Profile   ③ Create a new one

⑦ Connect   ④ Tick Anonymous

⑤ Set the Directory

⑥ Save the setup

Working at an FTP site

FTP gives you a two-way, interactive connection to the remote host. You can treat its directories and files as if they were in a drive in your own machine – almost.

● Downloading is like copying a file from another disk – but much slower. Be patient.

● If you want to upload a file, only do so into a directory that welcomes contributions – if you can't see one called UPLOADS, they probably don't want your files.

● Don't delete or edit files or directories on the Host – it shouldn't let you, but it might have let its guard slip.

WS_FTP options

There are a whole set of options that you can set to fine-tune WS_FTP to your way of working. Most can be safely left at their defaults until you have been using it for some time, but there is one that you should check.

It's very easy to double click by mistake. What do you want to happen when you do this? Go to the **Advanced** tab, and select the **Double Click Action.**

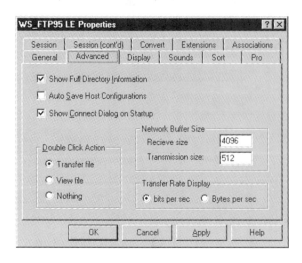

❑ Downloading

1 Change directory if need be – use the same techniques as in any File Manager.

2 Highlight a file that interests you.

3 Set the directory on your local system to receive a file.

4 Opt for **ASCII** to transfer text files, **Binary** for any others.

5 Click ← to download.

6 Use Close to return to the first panel and set up a new session.

7 Click Exit to end.

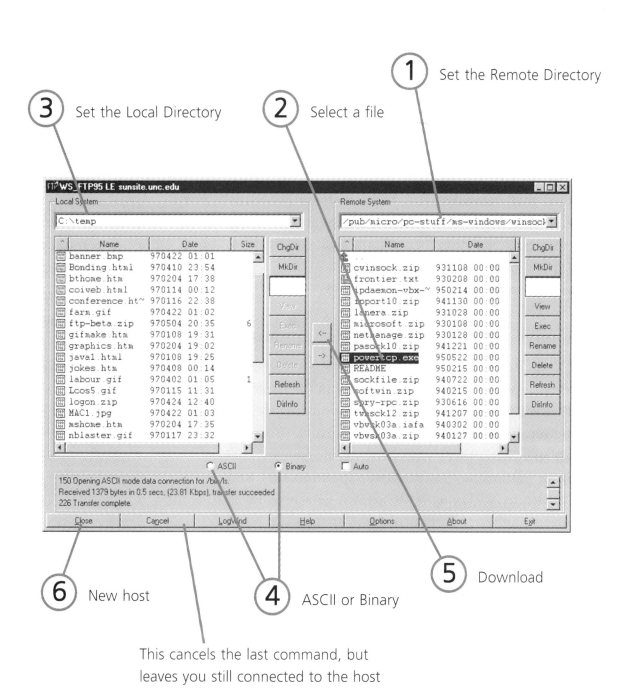

1 Set the Remote Directory

3 Set the Local Directory

2 Select a file

5 Download

6 New host

4 ASCII or Binary

This cancels the last command, but
leaves you still connected to the host

Archie

Browsing FTP sites is not an efficient way to find a file. You will find it far quicker if you know where to look, and for this you need Archie.

Scattered over the Internet are a number of hosts that act as Archie servers. Each of these has a database of the directory listings of major FTP sites, and a program for searching that database. The Archie servers know the names, locations, sizes and dates of last update of the files of those sites, though they do not know what is in the files, what type they are or what they do.

Search types

Archie can use one of four different matching methods as it searches its database.

Substring: Looks for the given string within the names of files and directories – and the more you can give, the better. For example, a search for Paint Shop Pro (graphics software) with '**psp**' produces nearly 100 hits, including 'crystalswa**psp**eedup.txt' and '**psp**lan.ps.Z'. Trying with '**pspro**' gets around 20 hits, including 'XD**PSpro**to.h', 's**pspro**g.txt' and '**pspro**40.zip' – the one you want.

Substring (case sensitive): As substring, but matching lower/upper case characters exactly as given. '**pspro**' would not find 'XD**PSpro**to.h' (good), but equally, '**PSPRO**' would not find '**pspro**40.zip' (bad).

Exact: Looks for an exact match (including case). This gets results fastest, but you must know precisely what you want. If you are looking for shareware or beta-test software, this approach may miss the latest versions. For example, the latest beta of Netscape at

108

Tip

If you do not know at least part of the name of a file, you cannot find it with Archie. In this situation, use a Search tool, hunting on the basis of its nature or field of application.

Take note

Regular expressions are case-sensitive – capitals and lower case letters are treated as different characters. If in doubt about which to use for a search, try lower case first – filenames are generally written in lower case.

the time of writing was '**n32e40b4.exe**', but searching for this now will give you an out of date copy. A substring search forf '**n32e**' will be more productive.

Regex: Use *regular expressions* when matching. These are similar to DOS wildcards. But not that similar – the differences are significant.

Regular expressions

The wildcard '.' (dot) stands for any single character. This was a rotten choice, as dot is an essential part of most filenames. If you want to use dot for its proper meaning – not as a wildcard – put a backslash in front of it '\.'

'winzip\.exe' will find the file 'winzip.exe'

'winzip.exe' will look for 'winzip**A**exe', 'winzip**B**exe', etc. and probably find nothing!

'*' is a repeater, standing for any number of whatever character was written before it. 'A*' means any number of A's. Use '.*' to stand for any set of any characters.

'babel.*txt' will look for files that start with 'babel', end with 'txt' and have something (or nothing) in between.

You can specify a set of alternative single characters by enclosing them in square brackets – '[...]'

'babel97[**ab**]\.txt' will find 'babel97**a**.txt' and 'babel97**b**.txt'

- Ranges can be defined with '-', e.g. [**A-F**] is the same as [**ABCDEF**];

- '^' at the start of a range means match characters that are *not* in the list, e.g. [**^A-Z**] means ignore all capitals.

Archie through the Web

To run an Archie search from your browser, go to Yahoo and select *Computers and Internet:Internet:FTP Sites:Searching:Archie.* There you will find a number of links labelled Archie Request Form or Archie Gateway.

1 Go to an **Archie Request Form**.

2 Enter the search string.

3 Set the **Database** to Anonymous FTP.

4 Select the **Search Type**.

5 Set the **Case**.

6 Start the search.

(1) Go to an Archie request form

(2) Enter the string

(3) Select the FTP Database

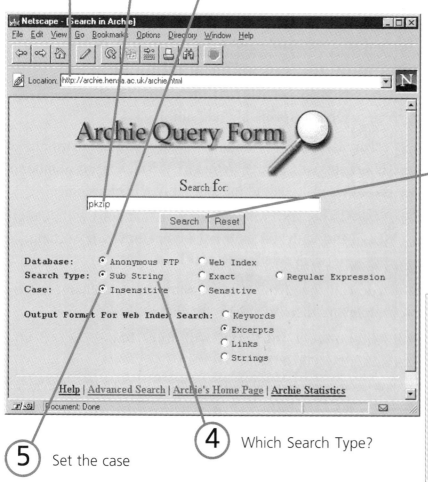

(6) Start

(5) Set the case

(4) Which Search Type?

Tip

The appearance of Archie request forms varies, but they all work in the same way.

Files from an Archie Gateway

7 Scroll through the results to find the file.

8 Click on a filename to download the file.

❏ If the site or directory is linked, you can jump there to browse for other files.

If your Archie search is productive, you will get a page or more listing the results. Here you will see the FTP sites, directories and name of the matching files. Sometimes all of these will be hyperlinked; sometimes there will only be a link to the file itself.

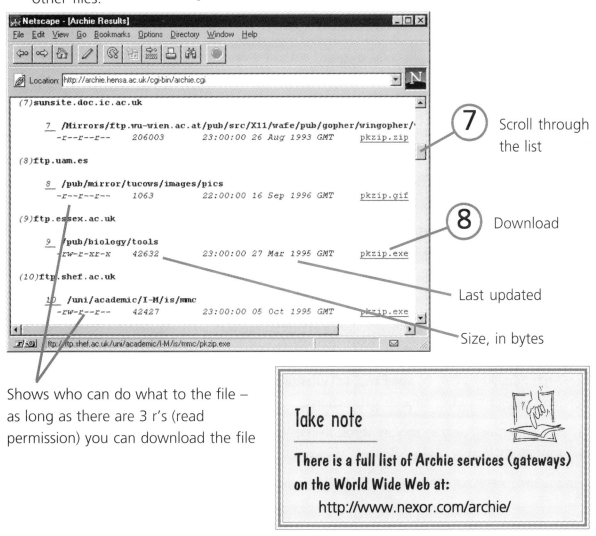

Shows who can do what to the file – as long as there are 3 r's (read permission) you can download the file

7 Scroll through the list

8 Download

Last updated

Size, in bytes

Take note

There is a full list of Archie services (gateways) on the World Wide Web at:

http://www.nexor.com/archie/

Summary

- ❑ c|net runs **Software Central**, where it holds shareware, commercial software and updates.

- ❑ **shareware.com**, another c|net service, has a large collection of shareware – and an excellent search facility to help you find the programs you want.

- ❑ One of the biggest organised collections of shareware is at **Jumbo**.

- ❑ **Tucows** has the most complete collection of **Winsock applications**.

- ❑ **ZDnet** has a smaller collection of good software and other files, selected with the home user in mind.

- ❑ If you are starting to build a software collection, the **Top 20 Shareware Gallery** at **clicked.com** is a good place to start.

- ❑ You can reach the **FTP sites**, travel through their directories and download **through your Web browser**.

- ❑ If you want to download files regularly, it is worth getting and learning to use WS_FTP. With this you can download faster and more efficiently.

- ❑ **Archie** is a program for searching for files in the Internet's FTP archives. It lives, alongside its database, on **Archie servers**.

- ❑ Archie searches can be for **Exact** or **Substring** matches, or can use **regular expressions**.

- ❑ You can reach **Archie servers through the Web**, and run your searches there.

7 Finding people

Finding e-mail addresses

As the Internet has no central controlling organisation, it is not surprising that there is no single, central Internet address book. So, if you want to send e-mail to people, how do you find their e-mail address?

The simplest solution is to phone them and ask. If they do not know their own address – and occasional users may well not have the details at their fingertips – ask them to send you e-mail. All mail software has, somewhere within it, a means of seeing the address of the sender.

If the phone-up-and-ask approach is not feasible, there are several databases of e-mail addresses on the Internet which between them cover quite a large proportion of users. Service providers often have member directories that other members can access to find addresses. We will cover a selection of these in this chapter.

Take note

The phone books run by the people-finding sites are US-only. Their directories of e-mail addresses, though geared towards the US, are more international.

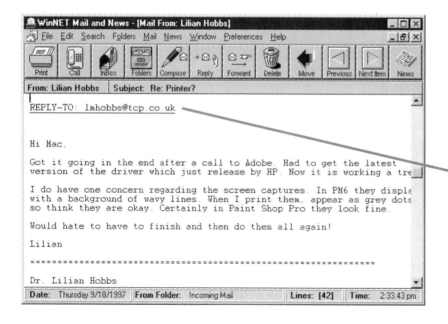

If you get e-mail from someone, you have their address

Basic steps

1 Go to WhoWhere? at:
http://www.whowhere.com

2 Enter the **Last Name**.

3 Enter the **First Name**, or at least an initial.

4 Select **E-Mail**.

5 Click **Find**.

cont...

The first place to look for e-mail addresses is at WhoWhere? It's quick, efficient and seems to have more addresses – especially outside the US – than its competitors.

There are two main problems you may have to deal with:

● Common names will produce far too many hits – you must find some way of restricting the search.

● First names can be written in different ways – full names, initials, nicknames. Even last names do not follow strict rules – are you sure of the spelling?

If the simple search from the top page of WhoWhere? does not give you what you want, you can refine the search at the next stage.

① Go to WhoWhere?

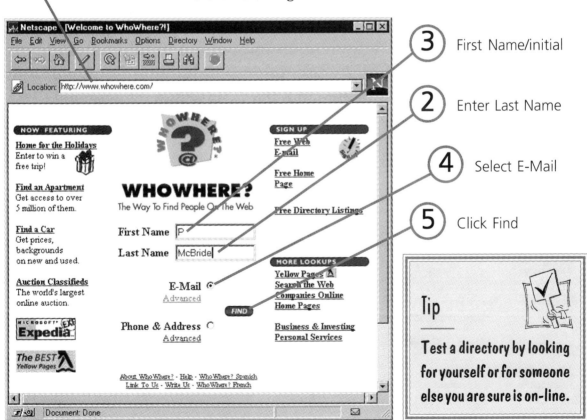

③ First Name/initial

② Enter Last Name

④ Select E-Mail

⑤ Click Find

Tip

Test a directory by looking for yourself or for someone else you are sure is on-line.

Refining the search

The standard search looks for an **exact match**, and will display those names which contain the given names exactly – so looking for 'P McBride', would find 'P K McBride' or 'Peter McBride' (if you are looking for me!) as well as any other person whose name started with 'P' or had 'P' as a middle initial.

If **all matches** is selected, 'P McBride' will also find any 'MacBride' and 'McBride' with different initials.

You can restrict a search to a **domain**. This could be the name of the service provider, if known, e.g. 'aol' or 'msn'. Outside of the US, you could useful give the country code as the domain.

❑ If you get too many...

6 Enter the **Domain** – the country code.

7 Select **exact match**.

❑ If you don't find it...

8 Select **all matches**.

9 Click **Search**.

> ## Tip
>
> **If you find several possible addresses, send an e-mail to them all – few people mind brief 'Is that you?' messages.**

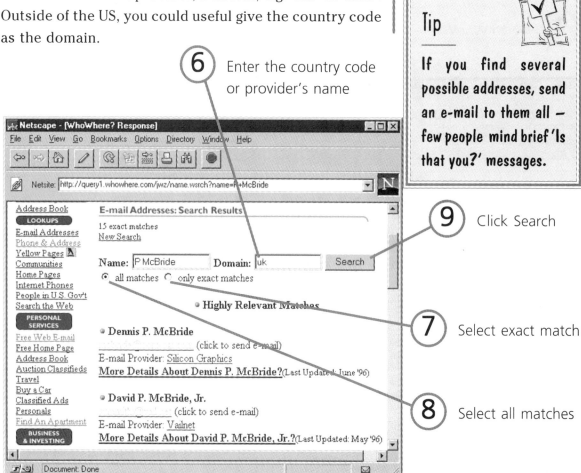

6 Enter the country code or provider's name

9 Click Search

7 Select exact match

8 Select all matches

Detour – Web e-mail

 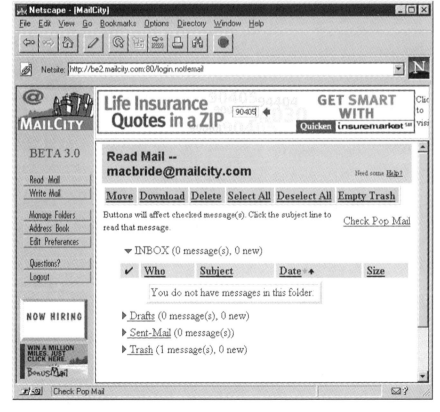
While you are at WhoWhere? you may like to take up their offer of free Web e-mail – the service is supported by advertising (on the site, not junk e-mail).

MailCity accounts are particularly useful for:

● people who access their normal e-mail through their business, college or other organisation, especially those who are away from their desk a lot. Web mail can be read and sent from any computer with access to the Web – not just your own computer on your desk at work.

● families, as each member can have their own mailbox, instead of sharing the one at the service provider's.

Handling your mail at MailCity is almost identical to working in Netscape or Explorer mail – the only difference is that you have to go to the MailCity site (and read the adverts).

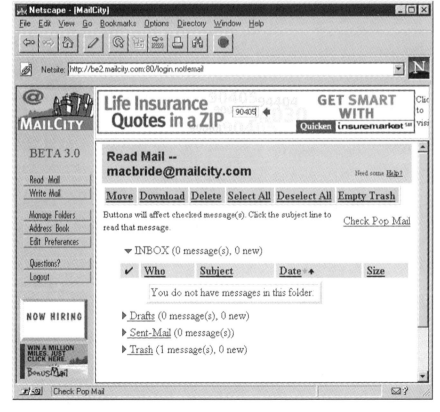

117

NetGuide

If you are a Netscape user, you have easy access to NetGuide, where you will find a choice of four people-finding directories. One of these is WhoWhere?, which we have already seen. The useful thing about working from NetGuide is that if WhoWhere? fails to deliver, you have three others to go at.

Let's start with BigFoot.

Basic steps

1 In Netscape, open the **Directory** menu.

2 Choose **People**.

3 Click on **Bigfoot**.

4 Select **E-Mail**.

5 Enter the **Name** – initial or first name and Last name.

6 Click **Begin Search Now**.

1 Open the Directory menu

2 Click People

3 Try Bigfoot

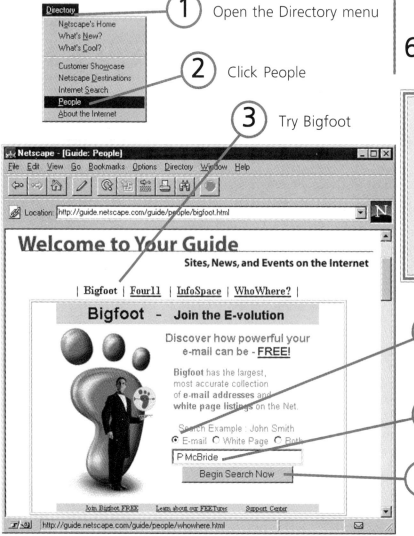

4 Select E-mail

5 Type the name

6 Start the search

> **Tip**
>
> **If you do not use Netscape, you can reach NetGuide at:**http:// guide.netscape.com

Basic steps

1 In Netscape, open the **Directory** menu.
2 Choose **People**.
3 Click on **InfoSpace**.
4 In the **Find E-mail** section, enter the **First** and **Last Name**.
5 Pick the **Country** from the drop-down list.
6 Click **Find**.

InfoSpace

The search form at InfoSpace asks for the first and last name, the City and State (in the US) or Country. As a result, if the person is in their database, you are more likely to find them first time here, than at either WhoWhere? or Bigfoot. Unfortunately, their database does not have particularly good coverage of countries outside the US.

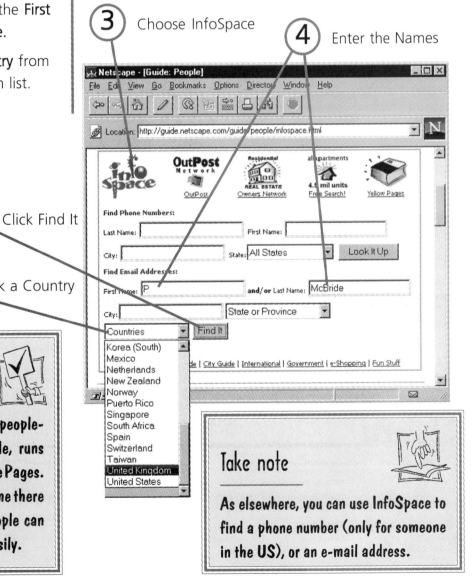

③ Choose InfoSpace

④ Enter the Names

⑥ Click Find It

⑤ Pick a Country

Tip

Four11, the other people-finder at NetGuide, runs the Internet White Pages. Register your name there so that other people can find you more easily.

Take note

As elsewhere, you can use InfoSpace to find a phone number (only for someone in the US), or an e-mail address.

Exploring for people

If you are an Internet Explorer user, Microsoft's Search the Web page would seem to be a good place to start looking for people. Use it with care! The search will return phone numbers and addresses – of all matching names in the US – as well as e-mail addresses of people on the Internet. So, give as much as you can of the name.

Basic steps

1 In Internet Explorer, open the **Help** menu and point to **Microsoft on the Web** .

2 Choose **Search the Web**.

3 Select a **White Pages** service in the bottom panel.

4 Enter the **First name** or initial – and **Last Name**.

5 Click **Search**.

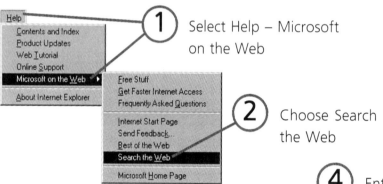

Select Help – Microsoft on the Web

Choose Search the Web

Enter the Names

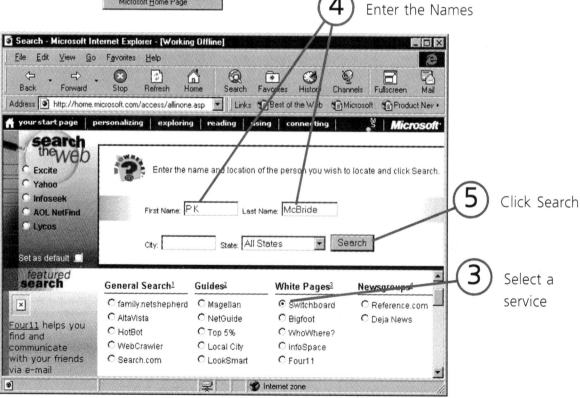

Click Search

Select a service

AOL's E-mail Finder

1 Go to AOL at :
   http://www.aol.com
   and select **NetFind**.

2 Switch to the **E-Mail Finder** page.

3 Enter the **First name** or intital – and **Last Name**.

4 Click **Find**.

Let's have a look at one last Web people-finder before we explore some alternative means of tracking down folk.

There is an E-mail Finder at AOL Netfind. It runs a simple name search, but at least you don't have to worry about geting swamped with phone numbers!

Find a Person is for US phone numbers and addresses

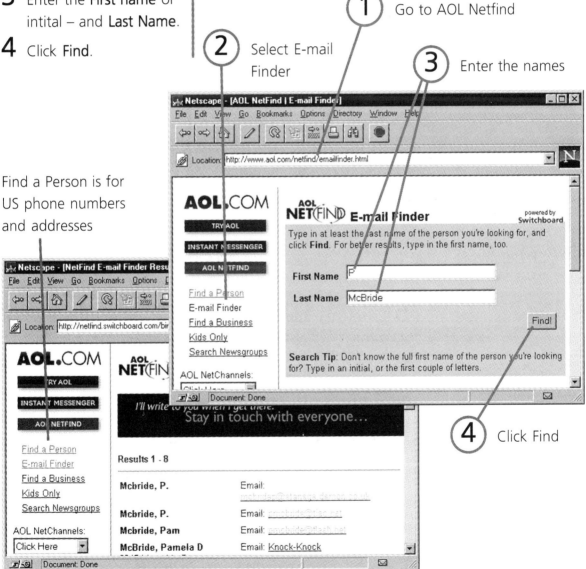

Whois

Whois is a standard tool on Unix systems with Internet connections. It can query databases held on Whois servers and – in theory – you can simply give a name and it will give you the e-mail address. In practice, Whois only works for those organisations that submit details of their users to the servers' databases.

WinWhois

This is another Winsock compliant program, like WS_FTP, so log on to the Internet through Trumpet Winsock (Windows 3.1) or Dialu-Up Networking (Windows 95) before starting WinWhois.

This compact and efficient piece of software is on the Net as 'winwhois.zip'. Amongst other places, you can find it at:

ftp.sunet.se/pub/pc/windows/winsock-indstate/whois/

Basic steps

1 Login through your **Winsock** software.

2 Run **WinWhois**.

3 Enter the **Name** – try the surname or surname, firstname.

4 Click Make Query and wait for the host to reply.

5 If the person you wanted is there, get the address.

6 Exit when done.

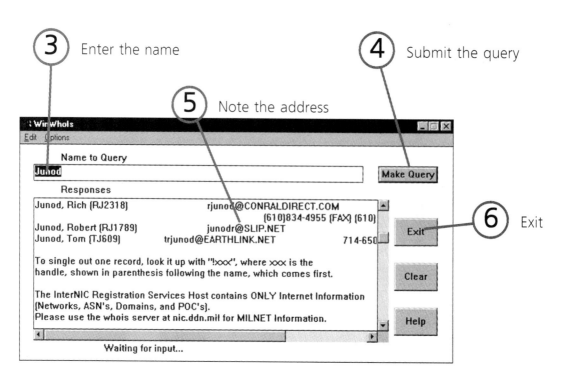

③ Enter the name

④ Submit the query

⑤ Note the address

⑥ Exit

122

Basic steps

1 Go to Internic at:
http://rs.internic.net/
cgi-bin/whois

2 Type in a name and
press [**Enter**].

3 Wait for the list of
names or a 'no
matches' message.

Whois through the Web

If you do not have WinWhois, or would like to try it out
before you get it, you can access Whois servers through
the Web.

There are links to half a dozen at *Yahoo*. Step through the
menus: *Computers and Internet – Internet – Directory
Services – Whois*. You can also go direct to the Internic
server through the Web.

 Go to Internic

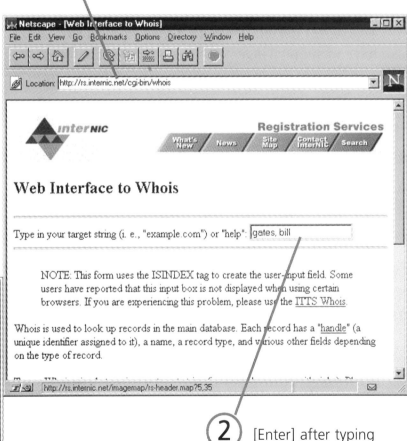

 [Enter] after typing
to start the search

Take note

Internic is one of the
central organisations of
the Internet. Drop in on
their site one day and
find out what they do.

Finger

Finger is a utility found on most Unix – and some other – systems. When prompted with part or all of a user's name, it will return more information on that person – including their e-mail address. Within a site it is often used to see whether or not someone is logged on.

Finger varies. On some systems a request to 'finger john' would tell you about all the people on that system with 'john' in their proper name or user ID. On other systems, you have to give the official user ID (which could be like this – 'cs1024jbs') to get any response.

When used over the Internet, rather than within a site, you also have to supply Finger with the name of the domain. You may have to know someone's e-mail address before you can finger them!

Your fingering may be in vain because:

● Some sites only give on-site users access to finger;

● Some computers do not have a Finger utility;

● Finger is case-sensitive on some Unix computers, so that 'smith' will not find 'Smith'.

To run Finger over the Internet, you will need suitable software, like WsFinger (opposite), or work through a Web gateway. You will find one at Yahoo.

Take note

Most computers will show a list of who is logged on at the time if you just type:

   finger @host

For example:

   finger@doc.ic.ac.uk

Watch out! A busy site, during working hours, can produce screensful of information.

Basic steps

WsFinger

❏ **Finger queries**

1 Click [Finger] to open the window.

2 Enter the query as *name@domain.*

3 Click **OK** to start the search.

4 If you get more than one match, scroll through to the results.

❏ **Whols queries**

5 Click [Whols] to open the **Whols** window.

6 Enter the **name**.

7 Enter a Whois **Host** – e.g. **rs.internic.net**.

8 Click **OK**.

This Winsock software gives a neat way to run Finger queries, and also offers a Whois facility – though as you have to enter the server name by hand, it is not as reliable or as easy to use as WinWhoIs.

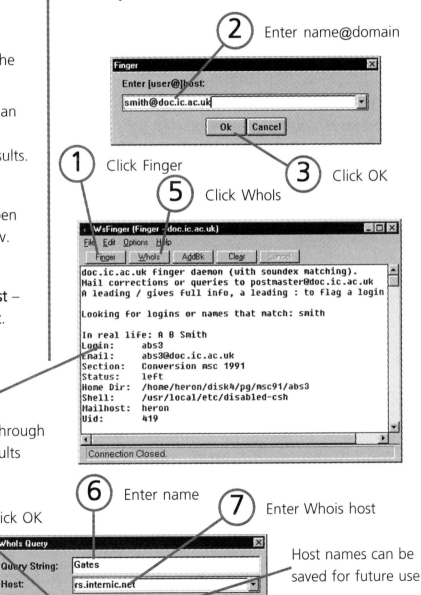

② Enter name@domain

① Click Finger

③ Click OK

⑤ Click Whols

④ Scroll through the results

⑥ Enter name

⑦ Enter Whois host

⑧ Click OK

Host names can be saved for future use

Member directories

Bigger organisations keep directories of their members, which other members can search. If you connect through a national service, it may be worth trying their directory when looking for a lost friend or other contact.

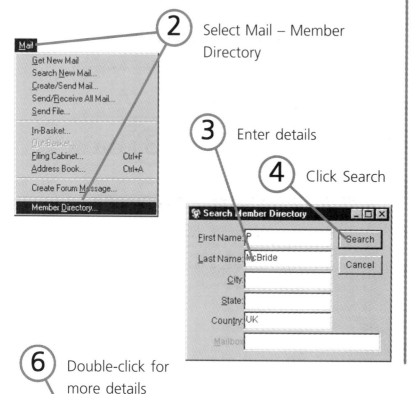

(2) Select Mail – Member Directory

(3) Enter details

(4) Click Search

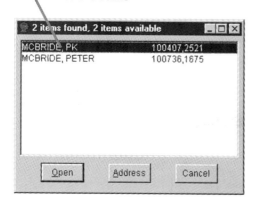

(6) Double-click for more details

Basic steps

- ❑ CompuServe

1 Log on to CompuServe.

2 Open the **Mail** menu and select **Member Directory**.

3 Type in enough details to identify the person – **Last Name** and **Country** may be enough.

4 Click **Search**.

5 If the search produces too many results, you will have to go back to step 3 and add **First Name** or **City** to narrow the search.

6 Double-click on a name in the results display to get fuller details of the person.

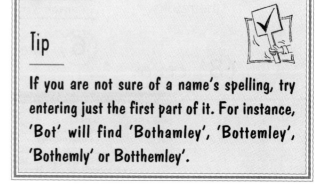

Tip

If you are not sure of a name's spelling, try entering just the first part of it. For instance, 'Bot' will find 'Bothamley', 'Bottemley', 'Bothemly' or 'Botthemley'.

Basic steps

□ **MicroSoft Network**

1 Log on to **MSN** and open your **Inbox**.

2 From the **Tools** menu select **Address Book**.

3 For **Show Names from the:** select **Microsoft Network**.

4 Open the **Tools** menu and select **Find**.

5 Enter known details on the **General** tab.

6 Click **OK**.

7 Click on a name in the **Search Results** list for more on the person.

① Open the Inbox

② Select Tools – Address Book

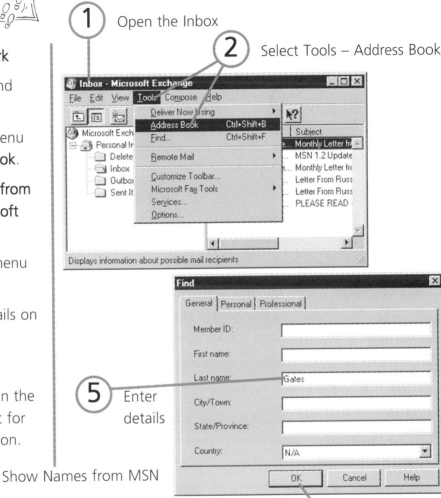

⑤ Enter details

③ Show Names from MSN

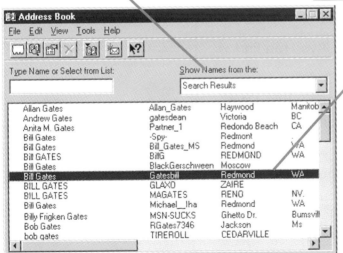

⑥ Click OK

⑦ Click for more info

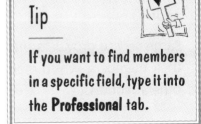

Tip

If you want to find members in a specific field, type it into the **Professional** tab.

Summary

❑ There is no simple, guaranteed way to find someone's e-mail address – the Internet just isn't that organised.

❑ **WhoWhere?** is the first place to look when you are searching for people. It holds the e-mail addresses of many people throughout the world, and also has access to the US phone books.

❑ Most of the people-finding sites – and some others – offer **free Web-based e-mail**. This can be useful for people who are often away from their desk, and for families who share one e-mail account.

❑ **BigFoot, Four11** and **InfoSpace** are good people-finding sites. These can be reached directly or through NetGuide at Netscape and the People search pages at Microsoft.

❑ There is a simple E-Mail Finding page at **AOLNetFind**.

❑ **Whois** can give you the address people working for those organisations that submit their e-mail details to the Whois servers – not all do.

❑ **WinWhoIs** is a Windows program that will handle Whois queries for you.

❑ Whois can be run through the Web – you can find **gateways to Whois** at Yahoo.

❑ Where a person is in an organisation that uses **Unix machines**, you can usually **Finger** them to find their address.

❑ Large service providers often maintain **directories** of their **members**, which members can use to find each others' addresses.

8 Using newsgroups

Searching Usenet

Newsgroups can be an excellent source of information – hints, solutions to problems, pointers to files and other resources. Some also circulate graphics, sounds, and other binary files. However, there are over 20,000 newsgroups, and many have over 100 new articles every day – efficient searching is essential!

Many search engines include a **Usenet** option when asking you where to search. The search is usually passed across to DejaNews which carries current and past articles from Usenet and other newsgroups. For extensive searching, or for more control, you can go directly to DejaNews.

Basic steps

1 Go to DejaNews at: http://www.dejanews.com

2 Type your search words or expression.

3 Click Find.

4 Click on an article's Subject to read it.

❑ For more control...

5 Select **Power Search**.

6 Set the options.

7 Click Find.

(5) Try Power Search (1) Go to DejaNews

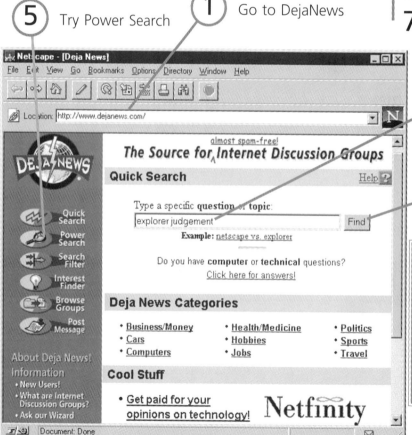

(2) Enter your search words

(3) Click Find

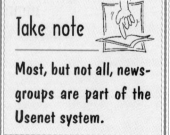

Take note

Most, but not all, newsgroups are part of the Usenet system.

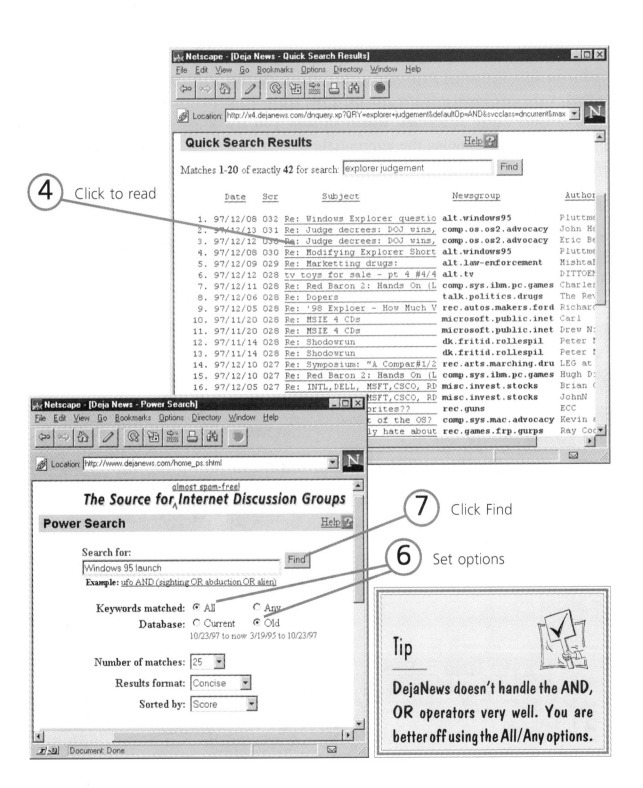

④ Click to read

⑦ Click Find

⑥ Set options

Tip

DejaNews doesn't handle the AND, OR operators very well. You are better off using the All/Any options.

Exploring the news

Searching all the newsgroups is a good approach when you want information on a specific topic – especially if it is likely to be discussed in many groups. If you are looking for a broader range of articles, within an area, you are probably better off finding the appropriate newsgroups and scanning their articles.

Outlook Express

Internet Explorer 4.0 normally uses Outlook Express to handle the mail and news. This has a neat routine for finding newsgroups – and once you have found them you can either subscribe, so that they are available whenever you log in, or just drop in to see what they have to offer.

1 Select Mail – Read News

4 Enter a name to find

7 Subscribe?

5 Select a group

8 Click OK

3 Switch to All

6 See what's there

1 In Explorer 4.0, click the **Mail** icon and select **Read News** or open the **Go** menu and select **News**.

2 In Outlook Express, click the **Newsgroups** icon or select **Tools – Newsgroups**.

3 Switch to the **All** panel.

4 Type a word to find in the newsgroup name and press **[Enter]**.

5 Select a newsgroup.

6 Click **Go to** to browse.

7 Click **Subscribe** to get its news regularly.

8 Click **OK**.

Basic steps

1 Select a newsgroup.

2 Open the **Tools** menu and select **Download this Newsgroup...**

3 Tick **Get the following items** then select **New headers, New messages** or **All**.

4 Click on a header to read the article.

Browsing the news

When you return to the main display, you must download the articles (or just the headers), before you can browse – just click on a header to open the article (you may have to wait for it to download).

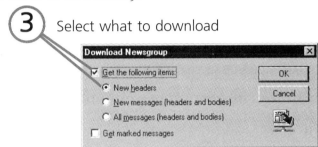

③ Select what to download

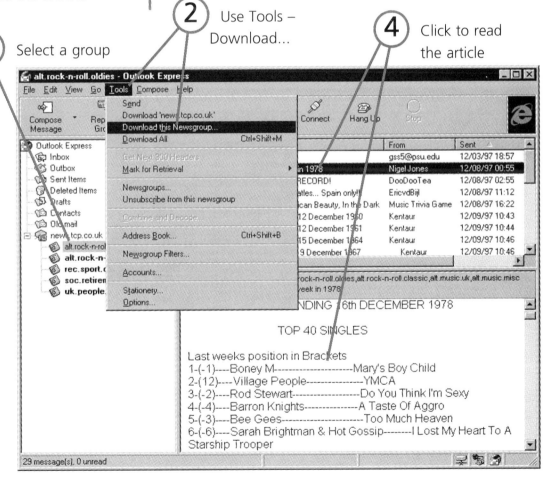

② Use Tools – Download...

① Select a group

④ Click to read the article

Netscape News

Netscape 3.0

In Netscape 3.0, the full list of newsgroups can be displayed. They are arranged into folders, according to the name hierarchy. As you open up the folders, you should see that Netscape is checking how many current articles there are in each group. When you select a group, Netscape normally start to download *all* its headers. If you only want a sample, and there are hundreds available, click the Stop button once forty or fifty have come in.

Basic steps

1 In **Netscape3.0**, open the **Window** menu and select **News window**.

2 Open the **Options** menu and select **Show All Newsgroups**.

3 Click on a folder to open it, repeating as needed.

4 Click on a group to download its headers.

5 Click on a header to download the article.

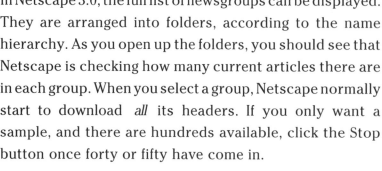

(1) Open the News window

(2) Show All Newsgroups

(3) Open the folders

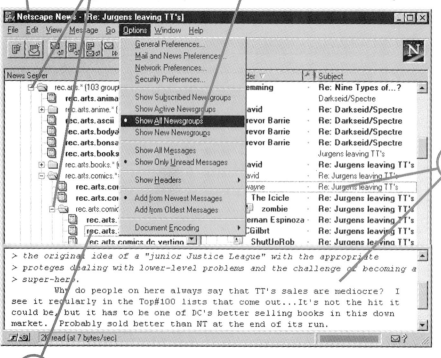

(5) Read the article

(4) Click to get the headers

134

Basic steps

Communicator's Collabra

1 In the **Message Center** click 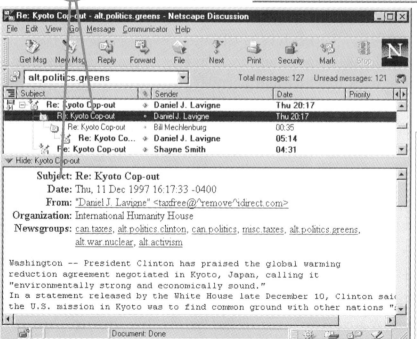 the **Subscribe** icon.

2 Switch to the **Search for a Group** panel.

3 Type a word to find in the newsgroup name and click Search Now .

4 Select a newsgroup and click Subscribe .

5 Click OK .

6 Read the news as in Netscape 3.0.

Collabra, handles newsgroups in a way that is more like Outlook Express than Netscape 3.0, except that you cannot browse a newsgroup without subscribing.

2 Open the Search panel   **3** Search for a name

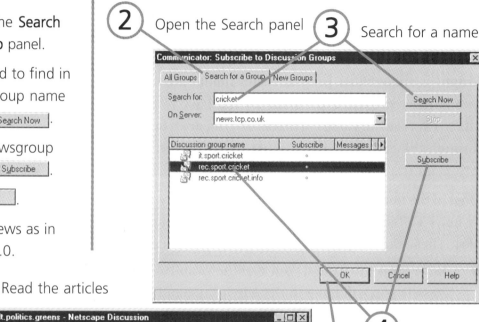

6 Read the articles

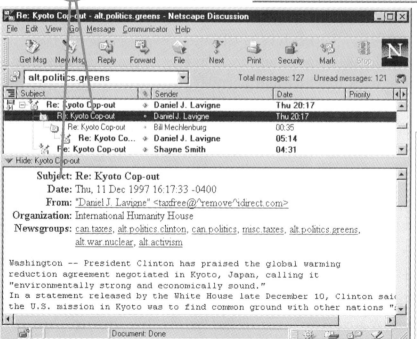

4 Subscribe to a group

5 Click OK

Tip

To remove a group from your subscribed list, return to the **Subscribe** panel, select it and click **Unsubscribe.**

135

Binary files

A key feature of the news (and e-mail) system is that it is based on 7-bit transfers. That is, the bytes coming down the wires only use 7 bits for data, with the eighth bit being using for error-checking. This is fine for plain text, as this only uses the first half of the ASCII set (characters 0 to 127) and these can be represented with only 7 bits.

Graphics, zipped files, programs and similar files – known as binaries – present a problem, as you have to use all 8 bits to express the values in these. To transfer a binary file through the mail or news, it must be converted to 7-bit format for transfer then back to 8-bit before it can be used.

Most of the time this presents no problems. Any good mail or news software will have routines for handling binary files. These do the job efficiently – with two exceptions:

- if the file is in a format your mail/news software can't handle you will have to decode it 'by hand'.
- Some systems put a limit to the size of articles and e-mail messages (around 60Kb). Larger files must be split into suitable sized chunks before transfer. You will have to stick these back together and decode them yourself (see page 140).

Here's how Netscape handles binaries.

Basic steps

1 Open the article and wait for it to load in.

2 If the article contains only gobbledygook, it needs decoding – see the next few pages.

3 If you can see the image right-click on it.

4 From the short menu, select **Save this image** – the **Save** dialog opens.

5 Set the **Folder**.

6 Type in a **Filename** *with the correct extension.*

7 Click **Save** and wait – the system may have to download the file again.

Take note

The Save File As.. options only include HTML and TXT, but don't let this fool you. Use the Text type if the file has been coded, otherwise just write the correct extension – GIF, JPG or whatever – into the filename. When you come to use it, you will find that the file is in the right format.

Multi-part files must be decoded

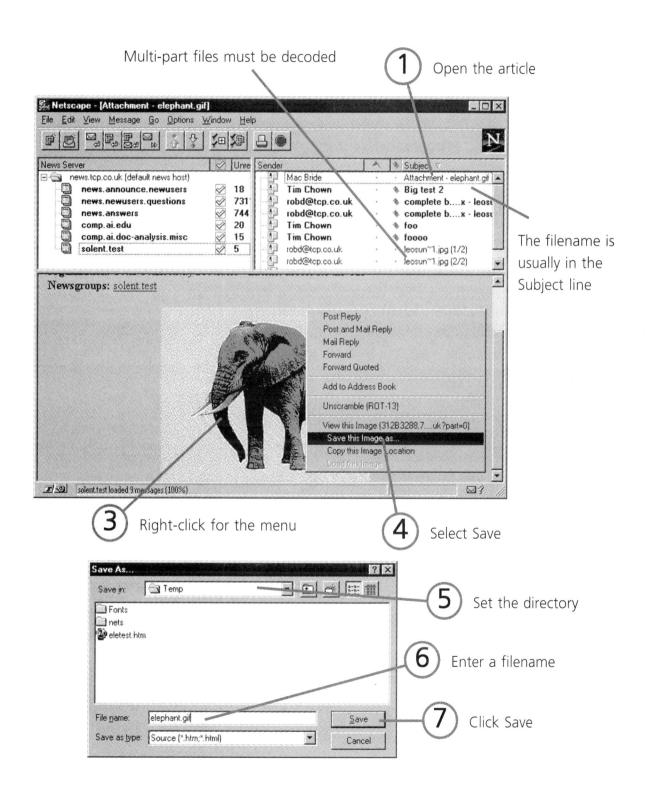

① Open the article

The filename is usually in the Subject line

③ Right-click for the menu

④ Select Save

⑤ Set the directory

⑥ Enter a filename

⑦ Click Save

Decoding binaries

Binary files can be represented as ASCII text in several different formats. The two most commonly used are **MIME** (see page 140) and **uuencoding**. To decode them you need special software, but it is readily available over the Net.

The decoding process is a bit long-winded, but normally straightforward. Briefly, you have to get the coded part(s) out of the article(s), joining them together if necessary, to create one text file. This is then passed through the appropriate decoder, which outputs the binary file.

Uuencoding

UU stands for Unix to Unix – a reminder that the Internet is based on Unix machines. Don't let this worry you – it works perfectly well on the PC. The decoding software is *uudecode.exe*, a DOS program. Your access provider should have a ready-to-run copy in their databanks. FTP a copy and store it in your DOS or Windows directory. Alternatively, there is a good Windows version that you can find at:

http://www.infocom.net/~elogan/wuudoall.html

Uuencoded files can be recognised by their first line, which always starts:

begin 644

This is followed by the name of the original binary file. The last line of the code is marked by:

end

Multi-part files will usually have breaks marked by:

- - - cut here - - -

Basic steps

❑ One-part files

1 Use the **File – Save** option to save the article as a text file.

2 Open the file in an editor and delete everything down to the 'begin' marker.

3 Delete any text after the 'end' marker.

4 Save the file – *as text.*

5 Run the **DOS prompt.**

6 Change to the directory containing the file.

7 Type:
uudecode *whatfile.txt*
(use its proper name!)

8 Check out the new file.

Tip

When cutting the coded part out of the article, make sure you include the 'begin' and 'end', but crop out any 'cut here' lines.

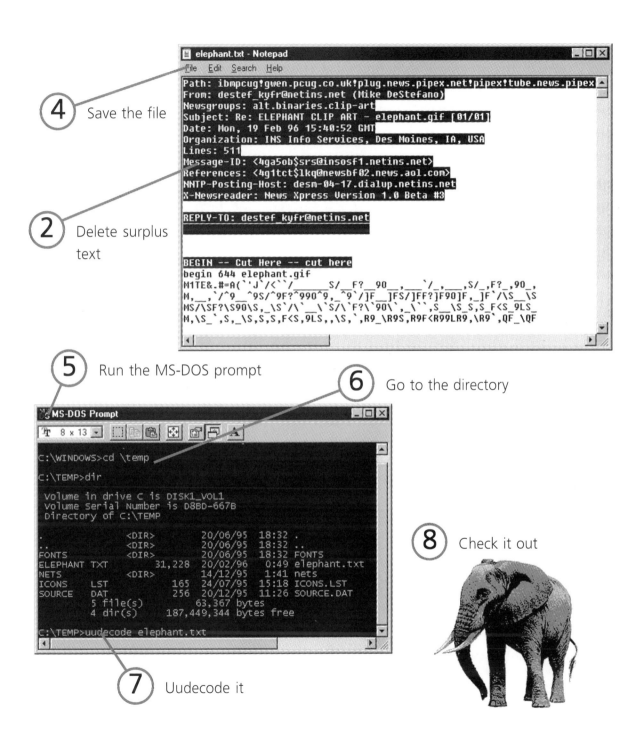

④ Save the file

② Delete surplus text

⑤ Run the MS-DOS prompt

⑥ Go to the directory

⑧ Check it out

⑦ Uudecode it

elephant.txt - Notepad

File Edit Search Help

```
Path: ibmpcug!gwen.pcug.co.uk!plug.news.pipex.net!pipex!tube.news.pipex
From: destef_kyfr@netins.net (Mike DeStefano)
Newsgroups: alt.binaries.clip-art
Subject: Re: ELEPHANT CLIP ART - elephant.gif [01/01]
Date: Mon, 19 Feb 96 15:40:52 GMT
Organization: INS Info Services, Des Moines, IA, USA
Lines: 511
Message-ID: <4ga5ob$srs@insosf1.netins.net>
References: <4g1tct$1kq@newsbf02.news.aol.com>
NNTP-Posting-Host: desm-04-17.dialup.netins.net
X-Newsreader: News Xpress Version 1.0 Beta #3

REPLY-TO: destef_kyfr@netins.net


BEGIN -- Cut Here -- cut here
begin 644 elephant.gif
M1TE&.#====A=@(='J'/<``/_____S/__F??__90__,___`/_,,___,S/_,F?_,90_,
M,_____^/9__^9S/^9F?^^99090^9,_^9`/JF___jF5S/jF_F90jF,_jjFF^/\S__\S
MS/\SF?\S90\S,_\S`/\`__\`S/\`F?\`90\`,_\``,__S__S_S_F<S_9LS_
M,,\S_`,S,_\S,S,S,F<S,9LS,,\S,`,R9_\R9S,R9F<R99LR9,\R9`,QF_\QF
```

```
MS-DOS Prompt

T  8 x 13

C:\WINDOWS>cd \temp

C:\TEMP>dir

 Volume in drive C is DISK1_VOL1
 Volume Serial Number is D8BD-667B
 Directory of C:\TEMP

.              <DIR>        20/06/95  18:32 .
..             <DIR>        20/06/95  18:32 ..
FONTS          <DIR>        20/06/95  18:32 FONTS
ELEPHANT TXT       31,228   20/02/96   0:49 elephant.txt
NETS           <DIR>        14/12/95   1:41 nets
ICONS    LST          165   24/07/95  15:18 ICONS.LST
SOURCE   DAT          256   20/12/95  11:26 SOURCE.DAT
        5 file(s)         63,367 bytes
        4 dir(s)     187,449,344 bytes free

C:\TEMP>uudecode elephant.txt
```

MIME

MIME stands for Multipurpose Internet Mail Extensions and is one of the standard techniques for transferring binary files through the mail or news systems. If you want to encode files into MIME format, you need MPACK – perhaps more importantly, if you receive a MIME file, you need MUNPACK to decode it.

MPACK and MUNPACK were written by John G. Myers (jgm+@cmu.edu). They are available for most types of machines, but note that the PC version is a DOS, rather than a Windows program. When hunting for it in FTP sites, look for ZIP files, with names starting 'mpack...'.

At the time of writing, the latest PC version was **mpack15d.zip**. This unzips into two programs, **mpack.exe** and **munpack.exe**. For ease of use they should be stored in your DOS or Windows directory, or any other directory that is in your standard path.

● You can use the same steps as for uudecode, simply substituting 'munpack' at the MS-DOS prompt. The steps shown here take a slightly different route to reach the same end.

❏ **Decoding one-part files**

1 Select the MIME message or news article, with its headers and use **Edit–Copy** to copy it to the Clipboard.

2 Open **Notepad** or any other word-processor and **Edit–Paste** in the selected text.

3 Save it as a text file.

4 Open the MS-DOS prompt and switch to the text file's directory.

5 Give the command: **munpack** *textfile*

❏ If the message contains a filename to use for the MIME part, that name is used for the output file. If not, the names 'part1', 'part2', etc will be used

6 Check the directory for your new file.

Tip

You can get MPACK and MUNPACK from:

ftp://ftp.andrew.cmu.edu:pub/mpack/

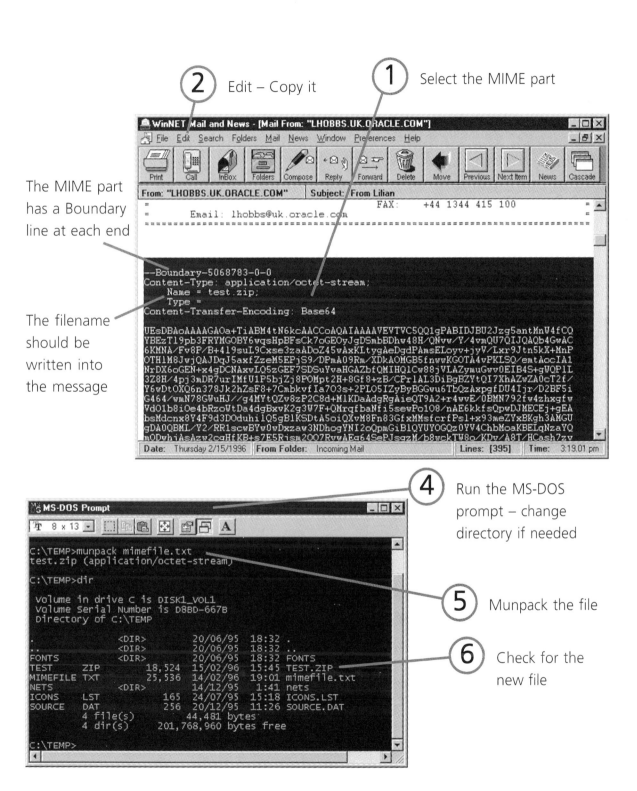

② Edit – Copy it

① Select the MIME part

The MIME part has a Boundary line at each end

The filename should be written into the message

④ Run the MS-DOS prompt – change directory if needed

⑤ Munpack the file

⑥ Check for the new file

Multi-part binaries

Decoding a multi-part binary file is simple – once you have amalgamated the chunks from the incoming articles. All you have to do is run the MS-DOS prompt and *uudecode* or *munpack* it. The amalgamation is the tricky part!

There are three likely causes of error:

- The parts are out of order – saving methodically will prevent this. The headers have numbers at the end to show how many there are in the set, and where the article fits, e.g. 02/05 is the second in a five-file set. One labelled 00/05 would be the accompanying description – don't save this.

- You have left line breaks or surplus text between the parts – check the joins. (If your first few amalgamations show that you can cut and paste perfectly, you can omit this from your routine.)

- One or more parts of the file has been corrupted – you cannot do anything about this, but fortunately it does not happen very often.

Take note

The amalgamated file will be too large for Notepad to handle. Stick them together in WordPad, Write or a word-processor. This will also give you the Find facility that you need for checking the joins.

1 Save the articles, with numbers in the names – 'part1.txt', 'part2.txt', etc.

2 Edit each article down to its coded text and save it again.

3 Open the first part in **WordPad** and move to the very end.

4 Open the next part, and make a note of its first 6 or 7 characters.

5 Select the text, copy it and paste it at the end of the first file.

6 Run the **Find** routine in your main file, looking for the first characters of the new part, and check that they follow directly on from the previous text.

7 Repeat steps 4 to 6 for any other parts.

8 Save the complete file under a new name – *as a text file.*

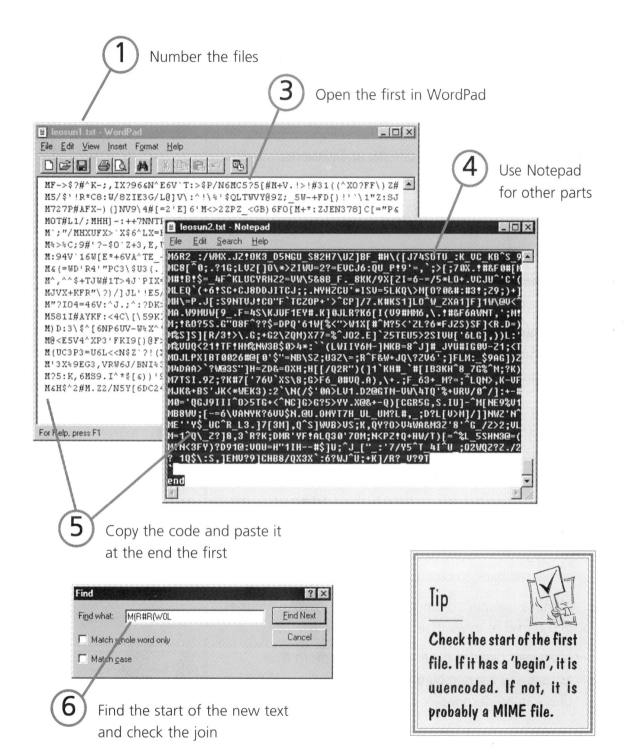

① Number the files

③ Open the first in WordPad

④ Use Notepad for other parts

leosun1.txt - WordPad

File Edit View Insert Format Help

```
MF->$?#^K-;,IX?96&N^E6V`T:>$P/N6MC5?5[#M+V.!>!#31((^XO?FF\)Z#
M5/$'!R*C8:W/8ZIE3G/L@]V\:^!\%'$QLTWVY@9Z;_5W-+FD[)!'`\1"Z:SJ
M727P#AFX-)(]NV9\4#[=2'E]6'M<>2ZPZ_<GB>6FO[M+*:ZJEEN378]C[="P&
MQT#L1/;MHH]-:++7NNTI
M'`;"/MHX-;(>X$6`LX=(
M%>>%C;9#',>?(-+>-$0`Z+3,E,'
M:94V`16W[E*+6VA^TE_
M&(=WD'R4#'MPC3\$U3(,)
M`,,^$$$+TJW#1T'PIX.
MJVX+KKxx@/JL.'!E5/
M"??I04=46V#[M=)$DL)J
M581I#AYKf;:4C\[\59K2
M)N;3\$^[6NP6UV-W%X^(
M@<E5V4^XP3'FK[i{j@f;:
M(UC3P3-U6L<<M$Z`?![(@
M'3X$9EG3,VRW6J/BXI%2
M?5:K,6MS9.I^^*$[&))'2
M&H#^*#M.Z2/N5Y[6DC2+
```

For Help, press F1

leosun2.txt - Notepad

File Edit Search Help

```
M6R2_:/WMX.JZ!OK3_D5NGU_S82H7\UZ]BF_#H\([J74SUTU_:K_UC_KB^S_9
MC8[^@;,?1G;LVZ[]O\*>ZIWU=2?=EUCJ6:QU_P!9'=,,`;>;[;7@X.!#&F@#[M
M##!B!$-_4F^KLUCYRHHZ2-UW\5&8B_F._8KK/9Y[ZI=6-=/5=LA>+JULJU^'C'(
MNLEE@+(+6!$SC+CJ8ODITCJ;;.NVHZVC)'*TSV=5LKK\>M[@?@&#?#[;?Z9;>+1
MMH\=P.J[[:S9NTVJ!C0'F'`TCZOW#+/7.K#KNS[]L@_W_ZXX1]F1W`@U<^
MMA_.W9MUW[9__.F-4%K[U+F#,K]J@J]JLJ1;PQ[I(U(9Z#M+#',[A';;T,;=-#;%6)[=:,#DH#8=-
MM;@(?;?!F#=K#;_R$_?^6__=V!W[#,#G7'5P%19=[:-^#M$'F!][%],['\G>U=6#
MM%S]S][R/#!<,;B.%G+[.*@2\Z@MK:++P(#+0[&?2GZ#/[+@?[:(&*#[S[
MM@UG[M.J!X=.[[#.*E7]Y4B[Z[RGJ[[C,8JG=/CO->[6/!@;%$&#>/_!@[Ł#[R+B[$=[A(
MM.JLUQIBBT@@26#@[@'$='==FH[SZ\=;:^F&H+JC:\ZV6':5]F:LM:_$9@G])Z
MM4DAH>`?=M@3S``]H&=T &@(/D=(]`FK&"D^D)ULM(;3KH8^T6%`}}ۘ[]3Mؓ`$U<>
MM7TSI.9Z;?K?K#7`[`76_'XS\8;/;=D_ @/HOL#$A]%=?A/_=F;@[[+LUSUY
MMJK/&+-+.P##J&I#,FK-(`<,#[/[W#[D<7-+:?[F)/[#[%ZW[LM/#5V_CۓM,/)/:+#&
MM/@-`"O@J 9IIIQ^0>5T$+<^NC]@/?5>>>>YY.X@&*-Q0)[CGR5G-S[IU]-^M[NE9%U
MMB58WJ[-+6-/-[.UAN1[.S#$_U$[#F3^_:#[L9[V]/>D;]Z][+S#+#IN[[VL.)`
MM/%[LS!;]/٣]-[L/_P[$%W[$[J2[W\+)/=#:;Q;`#[/$Z~>+/]/Z~/2
MM=-1@\_?Z]]@3]3^R?K+]$DM#+`3ûY#!/NQ;@[}7@M+;<PZ:!@+DW/;ꤩ]-ꚃM[[;#
M:M<3FY)?@91@:U@U=H"1LH--#$]U]^J_::'7/Y5^T_4I^U_;@2WQQ?Z./2
M?_1@$\:S,;]EEMU?9]]CHB8/QY:Z::+6::L^6WJ^*Z]/R^*K]/R?_U?9Q
```

end

⑤ Copy the code and paste it at the end the first

Find

? ×

Find what: M(R#R(WOL   Find Next

☐ Match whole word only   Cancel

☐ Match case

⑥ Find the start of the new text and check the join

Tip ☑

Check the start of the first file. If it has a 'begin', it is uuencoded. If not, it is probably a MIME file.

Summary

❑ The best way to get the flavour of a newsgroup is to **sample its articles**. You don't have to subscribe to the group to do this.

❑ You can search **Usenet** (and other) newsgroups at most search engines, or directly at **DejaNews.**

❑ **Outlook Express** is the mail and news system normally used with Internet Explorer. It has an excellent routine for finding newsgroups by name. You can then go to a group to sample its contents.

❑ **Netscape 3.0** has a **News** window with a full set of commands for handling news articles.

❑ **Communicator** includes the **Collabra** mail and news software. This lets you search for groups by name, but you can only read the messages by subscribing.

❑ There are usually **built-in routines** for **detaching binary files** from e-mail messages and news articles.

❑ Where binary files are split over several articles, or are in a format that the news/mail software cannot handle, you will have to **detach** them **by hand.**

❑ **Uuencoded** files can be recognised by the 'begin 644' message at the start of the file. These can be converted back to binary form with uudecode.

❑ **MIME** is another common format for sending binaries in the mail or news. Use MUNPACK with these.

❑ **Multi-part binaries** have to be cut out from their articles and reassembled in a word-processor before they can be decoded.

144

Index